Faith's Wisdom for Daily Living

Other books in the Lutheran Voices series

See *www.lutheranvoices.com*

LUTHERAN
VOICES

Faith's Wisdom for Daily Living

Herbert Anderson
Bonnie J. Miller-McLemore

Augsburg Fortress

Minneapolis

FAITH'S WISDOM FOR DAILY LIVING

Page 17: Michael Moynahan, "Litany of Contradictory Things," *Orphaned Wisdom: Meditations for Lent* (Mahwah: Paulist, 1990). Used courtesy of the Paulist Press, by permission; page 18: Pat Parker, "For the White Person Who Wants to Know How to Be My Friend," in *Movement in Black* (Ann Arbor: Firebrand, 1990), 99. Used by permission; page 22: 1 stanza from "Christus Paradox" by Sylvia Dunstan. © 1991 by GIA Publications, Inc. Chicago, IL All rights reserved. Used by permission; chapter 2 is adapted from, "Seeing and Saying the Other Side," *The Lutheran*. August, 2005, © 2005 Evangelical Lutheran Church in America, admin. Augsburg Fortress.

Cover photo: © John Coletti / Stone/ Getty Images

Library of Congress Cataloging-in-Publication Data
Anderson, Herbert, 1936-
Faith's wisdom for daily living / Herbert Anderson and Bonnie J. Miller-McLemore.
    p. cm.
ISBN 978-0-8066-5366-2 (alk. paper)
1. Theology, Practical 2. Theology, Doctrinal. I. Miller-McLemore, Bonnie J. II. Title.
BV3.A46 2008
248—c22
2007037230

Manufactured in the U.S.A.

12   11   10   09   08   2   3   4   5   6   7   8   9   10

Contents

1

Faith's Wisdom: A Meditation on Practicing Theology

This book responds to a simple question that can be asked in many ways: What is the connection between what we believe and how we live? Is Christian theology a resource for the decisions we make in the workplace, in our homes, on the run, in a world of competing beliefs and solutions, without time for careful reflection and research? Do we regard the Christian faith as a source of wisdom for daily living?

The book's content grew out of an invitation from the Evangelical Lutheran Church in America to deliver the 2005 Hein-Fry Lectures. For the first time, the planning committee for the lectures chose two pastoral theologians, inviting us to address a couple of intriguing questions:

Can theological ideas such as creation, sin, redemption—and particularly Lutheran themes such as law/gospel, the hiddenness of God, the theology of the cross, and simultaneously saint and sinner—be appropriated helpfully for Christian living today?

How do the current contexts for practicing the Christian life shape and reshape our understanding of these traditional theological categories?

Inviting practical theologians to reflect on theological themes and doctrine represents a watershed of sorts. We were asked not only to articulate the meaning of theological doctrine but also to identify its pastoral and practical value and how it shapes and is shaped by everyday life. The questions of the committee reflect a desire for what might be called "theological fluency" in Christian living, the ready and facile everyday use of language particular to religious traditions. Does our theology, they seemed to ask, answer the questions people are raising?

Many Christians today see theology as far removed from their own lives. They do not connect theoretical debates about the nature of God, the work of Christ, or the presence of the Holy Spirit and their daily problems. Instead, theology is viewed as an academic exercise for experts, something scholars do in the ivory towers of seminaries and divinity schools at a distance from daily routines and life's quandaries. It is not seen as a many-faceted activity in which they and others in church and society engage in different ways and for different purposes.

When practical theology is at its best, it invites us to take questions of human experience seriously. Martin Luther's desperate longing for a gracious God is probably not the burning question of our time. Instead, people ask: "Am I safe?" "Will I be included?" "Can I get what I want?" "How can I live wisely in a fragile environment?" These questions are not trivial. And they are compounded today by the complexities of life in a global society. They challenge us to rethink traditional categories and require answers that run beyond Luther's answer of justification by grace.

Luther's practical theology contains "untapped resources" for reconstructing such a practical theology, according to Niels Henrik Gregersen. In a way, our book is a response to Gregersen's proposal: "A classical Lutheran theology needs to be reconstructed in response to the new challenges that face the churches in a global, multi-religious world . . . [e.g.] the saving power of Christ, and not a doctrine of justification, is what must be believed."[1] Although this book does not rely solely on Luther, we hope it will begin a fruitful and long overdue exploration of whether and how he was a practical theologian.

Whereas systematic theology often focuses on the coherence or incoherence of beliefs, practical theology tries to monitor how people actually live out these convictions on a regular basis and, inversely, how this living out impinges upon belief. Practical theologians are interested in understanding theology "dynamically." That is, they study the "dynamics of theology" or "the lived life." Practical theologians run back and forth, one might say, between "academic theology" and "everyday theology."[2] This also requires a turn to a wide variety of sources—other fields in the study of religion (such as New Testament and ethics), disciplines outside religion (such as psychology and political science), and experiences and practices of people themselves. When we are able to understand doctrine dynamically, the wisdom of faith traditions take on modern relevance and ancient teachings are refurbished by the challenges of modern living.

In short, this book takes up the daunting challenge of moving back and forth between doctrine and everyday life. How can traditional theological categories inform faithful living today? What questions from Christian practice might reshape theological understanding? It examines both questions in terms of four themes or dimensions of the Christian life—ambiguity, frailty, sacrifice, and awe. In the original Hein-Fry Lectures, Herbert Anderson talked about ambiguity and awe, while Bonnie Miller-McLemore explored sin and sacrifice. Each chapter still carries the author's own voice and approach. Anderson identifies dispositions or affective attitudes that are an essential link between what people believe and what they do. Miller-McLemore examines ways in which doctrines come alive in, bear on, and are changed by daily practice. But both seek to discern faith's wisdom in the interplay between doctrine and daily living. The chapters have been rearranged slightly from the lectures to follow the natural flow of human experience from ambiguity and paradox (Chapter 2) and sin and finitude (Chapter 3) to love and sacrifice (Chapter 4) and wonder and awe (Chapter 5). Although all four chapters focus on both Christian problems and answers, the book follows a slight shift in emphasis from the challenges of existence (ambiguity, paradox, frailty, and sin) to some of the rewards and answers (love, sacrifice, awe, wonder, and grace).

We envision an audience of thoughtful Christians who struggle with these matters as they live out their faith. The basic presumption of the book is that every Christian—mothers, fathers, plumbers, cooks, doctors, teachers, truck drivers, clerks, and so forth—is a practicing theologian who must discover the significance of Christian wisdom for daily life. It invites readers to think about Christian theology and doctrine as a dynamic, living stream that informs faithful living today and in turn is reshaped by the questions we ask of the tradition out of present experience.

Wisdom is a word that deserves more careful theological consideration. We need to know much more about what constitutes it, how it comes about, and how it thrives. When we use the term, we point toward knowledge that lies at the intersection of the great traditions of the Christian community and everyday practice. Faith's wisdom does not simply reside in historical and contemporary doctrines but in its lived embodiment among those who profess Christ. Capturing and articulating how this happens is a challenging task.

One biblical commentary on wisdom in the book of Proverbs describes it as "a profound truth tested by the generations" or a "philosophy rooted in the soil of life," written to help the youth of its day "avoid all snares and dangers."[3] Theological and spiritual wisdom is not a mind-game that stands outside or above daily life. It occurs within it and requires practice, action, and concrete enactment. This moves us beyond theology as propositional or theology as propositions about the nature of God. Wisdom refers to a relational, spiritual, and theological knowing that is more than technique, information, or academic knowledge. It includes pragmatic guidance to Christian compassion and to building God's realm on earth. Wisdom is theological know-how of the best kind embedded in the practices, rituals, and routines of the deeply knowledgeable and faithful Christian.

For Reflection

1. How have you heard the word *theology* used? How do you understand it? Do you see yourself as doing theology?

2. What question or questions of faith plague you most centrally in the midst of your own daily family and work life?

3. How would you define Christian wisdom?

2

Embracing Ambiguity

In every age, the church seeks to provide wisdom to individuals and communities facing the ordinary problems of their particular situation. In our time, a shrinking global community and terror everywhere have intensified those problems. Encounters with differences that once were the province of missionaries, the adventurous, the open-minded, or those too poor to live where they wished, are now an unavoidable and irreversible dimension of daily living for more and more people. The worlds in which we live are increasingly less homogeneous and stable because we live in diverse and unpredictable global contexts. Of course, the diversity of religions and cultures is not new. What is new is that human difference is no longer hidden by geographic distance or religious and cultural imperialism. We no longer can assume a common worldview in the primary contexts of our lives.

As the everyday world has been enlarged and enriched by more and more diversity, certainty has diminished and fearfulness increased. People frequently are overwhelmed by too much ambiguity and too much uncertainty. Fear of difference fractures common ground and makes strangers dangerous. Because we participate simultaneously in very different social or cultural networks, we need to be formed to live with uncertainties, contradictions, ambiguities, and conflicting interests. We cannot assume that neighbors or even fellow church members will share the same worldview. Learning to honor difference and embrace ambiguity is an urgent agenda for the sake of peaceable human communities, the common good, and the world's future.

Connecting theology with daily life is seldom easy. Sometimes the gap between past Christian teaching and modern dilemmas seems insurmountable. What will connect Lutheran theology with practices of faithful living in the midst of so much diversity and uncertainty? Our proposal is that the *paradox perspective* is the distinctive contribution of the Lutheran Christian heritage for practicing theology in the midst of diversity and uncertainty. Connecting what we believe with how we act requires something more, however. That 'something more' is the soul's attitude formed in faith by the Spirit of Christ. Embracing ambiguity is an attitude or disposition of the soul that encourages paradoxical living.

Comfort in Absolutes

A few years ago, I experienced religious diversity as I began an early morning plane trip from Seattle, Washington. The cab driver who was to take me to the airport asked politely if I would wait two minutes. When I agreed, he spread newspaper on the sidewalk in front of my house, faced east in the morning darkness, and prayed. I learned that my Muslim cabdriver was from Eritrea and had come to the United States through the sponsorship of a Lutheran family in Moorhead, Minnesota. When I got to the airport the man sitting next to me in the waiting area, an Orthodox Jew in appearance, was reading from the Torah. I was keenly aware that it was 6:30 A.M. and I had not prayed yet, but my Muslim and Jewish brothers had.

Growing up in Scandia, Minnesota, in the 1950s did not prepare me to live in a world of diversity and ambiguity. Scandia was heavily populated by Swedish farmers. Most were Lutheran, Republican, and drove General Motors cars. Lacking even a Roman Catholic Church, the community I grew up in was even more homogenous than Garrison Keillor's mythical Lake Wobegon. The piety of my childhood was full of absolutes and rules to keep things and people separate. Cards with aces and faces or restaurants that served alcoholic beverages were unambiguously evil. So was dancing. Things were mostly this way or that. It was Eric Wahlstrom, my New Testament professor at Augustana Theological Seminary, who opened my eyes to a new way of seeing the world. In response to some question about interpreting a text, I remember Wahlstrom saying, "Vell boys," (and we were then all boys), "it could be dis vay and den again it could be dat vay and it really doesn't make any difference—bot are true." It has taken me a lifetime to live into those three words—both are true.

For anyone who remembers a time of quiet lives in common worlds, the safety of sameness and the presumption of certainty are seductive. Even those who have grown up with multiculturalism as the norm may still wish to live without the complexities of pluralism. Throughout human history, most people have lived in situations in which socialization processes were unified around a common view of reality and a shared vision of the good. It was easy to take certainty for granted. Pluralism guarantees that socialization processes are no longer uniform and perspectives on reality are many. The gift of diversity is that it enlarges our understanding of the world. The challenge of diversity is that there are fewer absolutes.

Living seems easier when we can assume people are similar and decisions are regarded as unambiguous. We would like to believe that things are this way *or* that way, that some things are true and some things are false. If democracy is right, other forms of government must be wrong. If capitalism is good, other economic forms are not. If heterosexuality is the norm, then homosexuality must be deviant. If Christianity is true, other religious expressions must be false. If two-parent families are best, then other family forms are unacceptable, and so on. When the desire to be more inclusive or when embracing ambiguity collide with presumptions of certainty or patterns of intolerance, conflict often follows. Culture wars have made neighbors into enemies, divided religious communities into opposing camps, fractured families, and colored some states red and some states blue. Whenever one side is absolutized, we are all the poorer for it.

The search for certainty and security in the midst of diversity and ambiguity has been deepened by a new awareness of human vulnerability in a time of terror. We have an uneasy sense, hidden deep in the human soul, that we are vulnerable creatures and therefore contingent and anxious. Instead of acknowledging that anxiety is an inevitable consequence of being vulnerable creatures, we are tempted to polarize the world so that we will have enemies to fear and fight. For anxiety we may take an antacid or an antidepressant. For fear we take deadly aim.

When our search for certainty is driven by fear, we are likely to become even more intolerant of ambiguity. We are inclined to perceive ambiguous situations as threatening rather than promising. When we lack information or experience or are uncertain about a life situation, we may seek control to avoid feeling uncomfortable. Looking for absolutes leads to an unending cycle of more and more intolerance and violence. And the person who interprets ambiguous situations as threatening is inclined toward intolerance of cultural or racial difference as well. The inability to tolerate ambiguity contributes to prejudice toward whomever or whatever is different.

Embracing ambiguity therefore is not just optional Christian practice. It is an ethical mandate.

The Inevitability of Ambiguity and Paradox

Intolerance of ambiguity will not make it go away. I mean by ambiguity the ability to understand in more than one way. When a thing is ambiguous, there is more than one interpretation or explanation. Ambiguity is rooted in the social character of all reality. The contradictions that are true are not accidental; they are inherent in human nature, in human community, in the circumstances of life, and in our theology. The deeper truths of our lives need contradiction or paradox for full expression. Humankind exists always and only in a relational web. There is a world that I fashion or construct, but there are also worlds created by others with which I must contend and over which I have no control. As a result, ambiguity is not just about uncertainty; it is about the inevitability of two-ness in human life, the permanency of contradiction, and the consequent possibility of alternative meanings. Michael Moynahan has written a litany of contradictory things that invites us to let the "contrarieties of the Lord" live and grow together.

> *Wheat and weeds:*
>> *let them grow together.*
> *Arabs and Jews in Palestine:*
>> *let them grow together. . . .*
> *Documented and undocumented aliens:*
>> *let them grow together. . . .*
> *The helpful and the helpless:*
>> *let them grow together.*
> *Wisdom of the East and West,*
>> *let them grow together.*
> *All contrarieties of the Lord:*
>> *let them grow together.*[1]

The litany may include more contradictions than any one of us could tolerate, but it provides a pattern for prayer as we seek to build bridges across the polarities of our culture and our church.

A paradox addresses deeper truths. The more we embrace ambiguity, the more likely it is that we discover contradictions that should not be resolved because they are true. Paradox is a self-contradictory statement or proposition that on further investigation may nonetheless be true. The task is to hold the paradox without choosing one side or the other. So, for example, if we focus only on our common humanity in a pluralistic world, we risk overlooking what is distinctive about "the other." But if we focus only on what makes others distinctive or unique, we risk setting them apart and stigmatizing them. In a way, paradox is systematic ambiguity. Neither ambiguity nor paradox should be confused with ambivalence. When we say we are ambivalent about this or that, we imply that we have contradictory attitudes or feelings and a pervasive sense of indecisiveness. In the midst of ambiguity and situations full of paradox, we still must decide and act faithfully in accord with our best discernment of God's purpose. Pat Parker articulates most clearly what I mean by a paradox in the opening lines of her poem "For the White Person who Wants to Know How to Be My Friend":

The first thing you do is to forget that i'm Black.
Second, you must never forget that i'm Black.[2]

Contradictions like the one expressed by Pat Parker are fundamental in human life. They are not to be resolved but to be lived with full awareness of their contradictoriness.

There are a number of ways to illustrate the centrality of paradox for being human. For the biblical writers, individual parts are interchangeable with the whole. Heart, soul, flesh, and spirit are equivalents for the whole person and vehicles of individual expression. So the psalmist can say, "My soul longs, indeed it faints for the courts of the Lord. My heart and my flesh sing for joy to the living God" (Psalm 84:2). We are from God and from the earth. Our dilemma as human creatures, as cultural anthropologist Ernest Becker graphically put it, is that we have the capacity to imagine ourselves a little lower than the angels only to be reminded that we are "food for worms."[3] Human nature is paradoxical because the human person has the ability for symbolic thought that transcends nature while at the same time being a creature that dies. Human communities like the family are equally paradoxical because being separate and being together are inextricably linked. We cannot exist without others who will recognize us and yet depending on the recognition of others is problematic because it seems to limit freedom.

Paradox is not only inevitable in life, but also positive for faith because it fosters humility before God and wonder in the presence of difference. Embracing ambiguity diminishes the divisions that our fear-filled absolutizing creates. Because cultural and religious diversity is on our doorstep and because we no longer can presume a common view of reality, we need to foster ways of living faithfully that will embrace ambiguity in daily living. A retired psychiatrist friend wrote this to me recently: "If I could add something to the drinking water in the United States, it would be a pill to promote the tolerance of ambiguity. It seems so much in our lives is determined by the need to find an answer when there is no answer."

The paradox perspective from the Lutheran heritage is an alternative to a pill in the water. It acknowledges the inevitability of contradictions in life and invites thinking paradoxically without being immobilized into passivity. Because our longing for certainty is so pervasive, striving to embrace ambiguity is itself, paradoxically, a necessary, yet unrealizable goal. Embracing ambiguity is a necessary practice of Christian faith because it deepens our awareness of the contradictions that are imbedded in life and faith. Embracing ambiguity is faithful Christian practice because it promotes humility and respect before "the other" who is different. Living paradoxically need not and indeed should not diminish convictions about what we believe is true. We simply hold those beliefs with humility because being a good neighbor trumps being right.

The Longing for Certainty

The longing for certainty is not new. More than fifty years ago, German theologian Paul Tillich wrote about anxiety in a way that accurately describes our modern condition. When Tillich wrote *The Courage to Be,* we were anxious about vague threats of destruction. In the 1930s, German fascism had developed out of the indefinite anxiety in Europe. That was replaced in later decades by a pall of anxiety over nuclear annihilation. That nuclear threat has now been

replaced by fear of concrete acts of terror by drive-by gangs and sui-
cide bombers. Our preoccupation with security has created a climate
in which fanaticism disrupts efforts at civil conversation, in which
gay is pitted against straight, conservative against liberal, in which
the freedom of the self is sacrificed for security and ideological
camps attack one another with disproportionate violence. Solutions
to our anxiety have become part of the problem.

When the spiritual center is gone, Tillich wrote in 1952, there
is emptiness and doubt: *"Everything is tried and nothing satisfies. The
contents of the tradition, however excellent, however praised, however
loved once, lose their power to give content today."*[4] The element of
doubt is a condition of all spiritual life because the human one is
always asking questions. The courage to doubt does not imply sur-
rendering convictions, but if we lose the ability or freedom to ask
questions, if fear trumps the willingness to doubt, there is no way
to access faith's wisdom without absolutizing it. Our inclination is
to flee from the freedom to ask or doubt and create a situation *"in
which no further questions can be asked and the answers to previous
questions are imposed on one authoritatively. In order to avoid the risk
of asking and doubting, the right to ask and to doubt are surrendered.
. . . Meaning is saved but the self is sacrificed."*[5] This is the greatest
challenge of our time. The freedom of the self to question or doubt
is sacrificed for the sake of certainty or we resort to fanatical self-
assertiveness to avoid ambiguity. When fanaticism takes root, people
attack those who disagree with disproportionate violence. The
inability to live with ambiguity and paradox is almost always costly
for the communal fabric.

Wisdom for Living with Ambiguity

The theological wisdom of paradox that will transform our terror into courage and our intolerance into the celebration of diversity is strengthened and sustained by the soul's resolve to embrace
contradiction and ambiguity as inescapable dimensions of faithful

living. Our proposal is that a paradox perspective is the Lutheran contribution for living in an age of pluralism and uncertainty. The centrality of paradox in Lutheran theology means that Lutherans live in a both/and rather than an either/or world. We will seek for truth and find paradox. We will long for certainty and find ambiguity. What is demanded by paradox is that we hold two things to be true that seem contradictory without looking for compromise. In another book in the Lutheran Voices series, *Public Church: For the Life of the World*, Cynthia D. Moe-Lobeda made this observation: "Recall the Lutheran insistence that ambiguity and paradox are unavoidable, and thus avoid any claim to know absolutely the correct Christian answer to the questions, or even the correct Lutheran-Christian answer for our time and place."[6] Living faithfully *is* living paradoxically.

The defining paradox for Lutheran theology is the conviction that the Christian is simultaneously righteous and sinful before God—*simil justus et peccator*. Other paradoxical dimensions of Lutheran theology will vary in terms of content but the form mirrors *simil justus et peccator* as *the* descriptive statement about the human person in relation to God. We are no longer what we were created to be and yet we are at the same time not yet what we shall become. We are responsible agents in a narrative that is written by God and others. *Simil justus et peccator* is a guard against the threat of despair because of persisting human sin from the one side *and* a guard against the danger of false security in God's grace on the other side. If we understand paradox at the center of faith, we will avoid absolutizing anything but God's grace.

The entire life of Jesus embodied paradox. The infinite became finite while remaining infinite; an ignominious suffering and defeat on a cross is in fact a glorious victory; a very specific event in space and time in relation to a particular people has significance that transcends space and time and a particular people; those who follow Jesus will find life by losing it; if we follow Jesus, we are free lords of all, subject to none and dutiful servants of all; our salvation is totally a gift from God that we must work out with fear and trembling. The parables of Jesus are troubling precisely because they go against the grain of a tidy mind and challenge our dreams of life without contradiction. A hymn by Sylvia Dunstan (1955–1993) titled "Christus Paradox" summarizes the paradoxical nature of Jesus in poetic form.

> *You, Lord, are both Lamb and Shepherd.*
> *You, Lord, are both prince and slave.*
> *You, peacemaker and sword-bringer*
> *Of the way you took and gave.*
> *You, the everlasting instant;*
> *You, whom we both scorn and crave.*[7]

The cross is the greatest paradox of all: to live we have to die. To walk the way of the cross, author and educator Parker Palmer once observed in a little book called *The Promise of Paradox*, "is to allow one's life to be torn by contradiction and swallowed up in paradox, it is to live in the reality of resurrection, in the sign of Jonah."[8] The cross, "calls us to recognize that the heart of human experience is neither consistency nor chaos, but contradiction."[9] Making the sign of the cross on the forehead of an individual being baptized is simultaneously a gracious promise and a dangerous act because it is an invitation to living paradoxically. It is the Jesus way.

Walking the way of the cross means that we are aware that God is always moving among us, unsettling illusions of certainty by which we live and creating transformative contradictions. Embracing ambiguity and paradox illumines the dangers of absolutizing anything but God's grace. Danish theologian Niels Henrik Gregersen has identified this paradox perspective as a challenge for Lutherans: "The capacity for living with contradictions rather than in neat uniform schemata may be an important stress test of a

Lutheran spirituality."[10] Lutheran theology, it is often said, is held together by the word *and*. All human beings are sacred *and* none are good. We live fully "in the world" *and yet* we are not "of the world." We are from God *and* from the earth. The contradictions we encounter simultaneously in diverse social or cultural or religious networks regularly challenge us to live more deeply into that paradox perspective.

Keeping a paradox like *simil justus et peccator* in view for daily living is hard work. Being made righteous or "just" before God by grace is difficult to sustain a world in which one is justified by performance and expected to earn his or her way. Taking this paradox seriously means that every work, every conversation with friend or stranger, every effort on behalf of justice begins with a word of grace. We are simultaneously sinners needing God's forgiving love again and again as we live our baptism *and* we are graciously forgiven people of faith who seek more and more to live out our baptisms. It is easier to live on one side or the other of that central paradox. To walk the way of the crucified and resurrected Christ is to remember our baptisms and the promises spoken there while we strive day by day, again and again against sin through God's mercy. We live in the graced conviction that how we practice the Christian life matters a lot and matters not. *The Jesus way is a contradiction to be lived with joyful gratitude and fierce struggle.*

Embracing Ambiguity as an Attitude of the Heart

Theologian Amy Plantinga Pauw makes the claim that "desires and dispositions play a key role in connecting beliefs and practices."[11] Attributes of the heart or dispositions of the soul are a necessary link between what we believe and how we practice our theology. The Christian story is replete with people who struggled, often unsuccessfully, to practice what they believed. If the recovery of faith's wisdom for living paradoxically is to provoke faithful yet critical Christian living, it must take spirituality or piety seriously for the sake of an integrated life of faith. "Dispositions of the soul" are like inclinations to human action that have been motivated and tutored by the Spirit of Christ.

The reluctant prophet Jonah is a good example of someone whose soul's disposition kept him from putting his good theology of mission into practice. Jonah's problem was not bad theology but the absence of desire to do the right things for the people of Nineveh. Because Jonah resented the truth of what he knew about God's merciful nature, he ignored the call from God and avoided practicing his theology. Even when Jonah decided to go to Nineveh, there was very little joy in his soul. The story of Jonah echoes the experience of many believers, as Pauw observes: "Religious attitudes and emotions exert enormous resistance against our best efforts at integrity between beliefs and practices."[12] The reluctance of Jonah illustrates how the disposition of the soul is the critical but sometimes fickle connection between belief and practice. It also demonstrates the necessity for ongoing transformation of the soul's affections. Unless they are tutored by belief-filled practices, attitudes of the soul will not automatically connect what we believe with how we act.

Religious practices like daily prayer, weekly worship, keeping Sabbath, sharing resources, and singing give direction to human desires and attitudes. These practices are from God and for God. They are God-shaped and God-shaping, divine instruments of transformation. In our worship practices, for example, the paradox perspective is reflected in the contradiction of *kenosis* (literally, "emptying out") and *plerosis* ("filling up"), of power and powerlessness, of fulfillment and struggle, of brokenness and wholeness. Theologian Gordon Lathrop uses the word *juxtaposition* to identify a liturgical paradox: thanksgiving next to lament, judgment alongside grace, speech with silence, the presence of absence beside the absence of presence. It is a way of challenging triumphalistic or elitist certainty or arrogance on the one side and immobilizing pessimism on the other. Human suffering is juxtaposed to ritual beauty: ordinary things of water, bread, and wine are juxtaposed to divine promise.[13] If our patterns of worship embody paradox, they will deepen our ability to live faithfully before God in an uncertain world.

Saying the Other Side

The connection between beliefs, practices, and dispositions of the soul is a circular one. One might begin that circular process with any one of the three but all three are necessary to fashion souls sturdy enough to live with ambiguity and paradox and make choices in daily living driven not by fear but by courage and compassion and grace. We have suggested that paradox, a central theme in Lutheran theology, shapes and is shaped by the soul's embrace of ambiguity and tutored by Christian practices of worship and prayer. The question that we must ask now is what practices embody the paradox perspective in daily life. Our proposal is that "saying the other side" is a necessary act of faithful living for a time of diversity, grounded in the "two-ness" or paradox of truth, and sustained by the soul's embrace of ambiguity. By "saying the other side," I mean the willingness to listen carefully and then say clearly another's point of view that is different than my own. It is an act of respecting that begins with wonder toward the uniqueness of "the other."

If the deeper truths of human life and faith need paradox for full expression and if it is most unlikely that we will choose paradox if we can avoid it, then saying the other side is a necessary practice for living faithfully in the midst of uncertainty. Because we are emotionally wedded to our deep metaphors and preferred absolutes and favorite narratives, we are reluctant to acknowledge with our children or with our spouse or with close friends or with colleagues at work that most every story has at least two sides. In order to honor difference and the contradictions that follow from living with diversity, we need to be intentional about seeing and then about *saying* the other side.

Saying the other side is a practice of Christian faithfulness that is necessary in order to discover the whole story or honor difference or live the questions of life and faith that only God can answer. Seeing or hearing the other side presumes, of course, that there is another side. In order to believe there is another side, we will need to suspend disbelief in the possibility of alternative visions. Seeing the other side is of course the first step, but we also need to say the other side in order to demonstrate a way of understanding that honors difference and embodies respect. Instead of drawing lines or making distinctions that separate, saying the other side invites us to explore the other side of everything.

Obviously, saying the other side must be done respectfully and carefully and preceded by careful listening. Saying the other side demands that we nurture the ability to hold in tension differing and even contradictory worldviews without needing to judge prematurely or draw rational conclusions. When judgments must finally be made, they will occur in an environment without domination and with respect for difference. Saying the other side in situations of care presumes that the goal is not to eliminate ambiguity but help people live the questions and the contradictions of life and faith. In that sense, it provides a framework for moral reflection without moralizing, for making judgments without being judgmental. Saying the other side does not require that we give up firmly held convictions or change our preferred view of a story. It simply fosters humility about the certainty of our view, honors others with differing views, and promotes a willingness to live with ambiguity.

If saying the other side is done in good faith, we need to be prepared for the possibility of being changed. If nothing else, our understanding of what it means to be human is enlarged by the stories we hear or the alternative perspectives we acknowledge. Being willing to be moved by another's story or another's thought reduces conflict in marriage, introduces compassion into every human interaction, and guards against domination of any kind. Not all sides have equal merit. We may discover that some have little merit. However, we don't know that when we first encounter difference of any kind.

We may eventually decide that the other side or even our side is in error or problematic in some other way. Saying the other side simply invites us to consider alternative views as a way of honoring human uniqueness and discovering a deeper understanding of life's contradictions through respectful listening.

Saying the Other Side in Practice

The ability to live with ambiguity and paradox in matters of faith is a challenging developmental accomplishment. Two decades ago, James Fowler acknowledged this difficulty with his idea of conjunctive faith in his book, *Stages of Faith*. Conjunctive faith is unusual before mid-life when the boundaries of the self that were once clearly defined are now porous and permeable. "Alive to paradox and the truth in apparent contradictions, this stage strives to unify opposites in mind and experience. It generates and maintains vulnerability to the strange truths of those who are "other."[14] Conjunctive faith, as Fowler has described it, is insufficiently certain for people who are fearful of ambiguities. The Christian practice of saying the other side creates an environment in which people in all stages of faith and all circumstances of power will feel comfortable saying what they believe *and* safe enough to imagine another possibility.

The paradoxical character of family is sustained by the practice of seeing and then saying the other side. Marriages that endure and flourish have achieved a kind of mutual recognition (seeing) between husband and wife that acknowledges (saying) each one as a unique and separate subject. Couples who are comfortable with the paradox of marital intimacy and distance will work toward forming families in which commitment to the whole and commitment to each separate person are held as a sacred trust. The family celebrates community and promotes autonomy. Children are welcomed, loved, and cared for in order to let them go. We leave our families of origin in order to go home again. If a family's belief system includes paradox at the center, it will embrace contradiction, ambiguity, and uncertainty as part of life and not alien to becoming family and being a faithful Christian.[15]

Those who have power are particularly obligated to practice saying the other side to insure that the silent voices are heard and contributions from the marginalized in our homes, our churches, and in the workplace are heard and taken seriously. Saying the other side creates a safe environment in which people of all stages of faith and all circumstances of power feel comfortable enough to say what they believe or fear or wish for *and* feel comfortable enough to imagine a point of view other than their own. In order to foster such an environment, saying the other side requires that leaders have what psychologist Newton Malony calls "double vision"—balancing short term needs and long term goals, being simultaneously idealistic and practical long enough to avoid easy answers, and valuing both sides of the paradox at the same time.[16] Although negotiation or compromise may eventually be necessary, a leader with "double vision" is one who can value both sides of a conflict long enough to deter negative polarizing or destructive absolutizing of either side.

The implications of saying the other side in situations of care are obvious but difficult to actualize. It presumes there is more than one side to the tension or conflict with a spouse or a child or a parent. Obviously, saying the other side must be done respectfully and gently. Careful listening and accurate empathy must precede it. No one is likely to consider an alternative vision unless they are first convinced that the position they hold has been heard and understood. Walking beside the person who lost the last argument is a way of making sure that the other side of the story is told and heard. Saying the other side also presumes that we need not eliminate ambiguity but help people live the questions and the contradictions only God can resolve. Saying the other side is not only an act of faithfulness; it is a sign of hope for a polarized world.

By Faith Alone

The Danish philosopher Søren Kierkegaard observed that a thinker without paradox is like a lover without feeling. Contradiction and paradox are inevitable dimensions of life and faith. We will seek for truth and find paradox. We will long for certainty and find ambiguity. It has always been so for those who seek truth. Abram left home and a familiar name for an uncertain journey to an unknown Promised Land. Moses left the tense security of Egypt for the wild uncertainty of a desert journey. The story of faith is finding security in the world of uncertainty, leaving the security of what is familiar for a world of uncertainty in which we discover real security that endures in God. The gracious love of God is certain even when our experience of God's love is not.

In a time when there are so many competing and even conflicting voices claiming to speak truth, there is an understandable longing for a faith perspective without doubt. Words like *certainly*, *certainty*, and *certitude* imply the absence of doubt, of being sure, or existing in fact and truth. Luther invites this confidence at the conclusion of each explanation to three articles of the Apostles' Creed with the statement "This is most certainly true." There are, however, alternate dictionary renderings of certainty that focus on reliability and dependability. The value of that definition for faith is that it shifts the focus away from abstractions of truth to a relationship with God who is reliable and can be trusted. The dependability of God and reliability of others are particularly necessary in the midst of ambiguity and paradox and are not impeded by uncertainty.

The unexpected gift of uncertainty is faith. There is no certainty other than the persistent and consistent grace of God and that is enough. By God's grace we live by faith alone (*sola fide*) with God the only certainty. All efforts at absolutizing anything other than God are challenged by Luther's understanding of *sola fide*. We are free to commend all others who are different to God whose grace and love is more encompassing than we can possibly imagine.

Embracing ambiguity in an uncertain and diverse world leads us to the centrality of faith and then from *sola fide* to the courage to live God's promise in the midst of so much uncertainty and wondrous diversity. *Sola fide* is the untapped gift of Luther's quest for a gracious God because it not only accepts uncertainty as the human condition before God, but also declares it to be good. It is an invitation to faith without props, faith without any certainty but the graciousness of God. This is enough.

For Reflection

1. Family therapists sometimes use the phrase, "the difference that makes the difference," to identify a problematic experience of otherness. Years ago, a father told me that if his son came home from college with a pierced ear, the young man would have to sleep in the garage. What experience of difference tips you over the edge? Where do we learn that difference is dangerous?

2. Contradictions are everywhere. Some of them are easier to live with than others. What paradox of faith is the most difficult to you to tolerate?

3. In his encounter with the persistent Canaanite woman who pleaded on behalf of her daughter, Jesus was changed (see Matthew 15:21-28). His assumptions about who was "one of us" and "who was not" were transformed. Most of us have had an encounter with a stranger who changed our perception of who is "the other." Who has been the Canaanite woman in your life?

4. The church I attend, Shepherd of the Hills Lutheran Church in Berkeley, California, begins worship with a statement that includes these words: "Welcome to people of every age and size, color and culture, ability, sexual orientation, to old and young, to believers and questioners, and questioning believers." How is diversity welcomed and honored where you worship?

3

Facing Frailty

"It's not popular to talk about sin any more," remarked a member of my church recently. He is right. Sin is not exactly part of everyday vocabulary.

There are good reasons for the silence. Talking about sin is disconcerting. It draws attention to our faults and failures. It reminds us of our own pain and suffering at the hands of those we love and whom we thought loved us. All this surfaces other emotions closely linked with the ache of sin—guilt and shame for sure, but also anger, grief, mourning, and lonesomeness.

As if this emotional upheaval was not enough, we are now more aware than ever before of the distortion in Christian views of sin. Many of us have bad memories of the misuse of the language of sin in our families and congregations. Christian claims about sin have done more than their fair share of damage, especially in relationship to children, women, and other vulnerable populations. The clever and the powerful have used sin and fear of punishment and damnation as one of the key ways to control people in both private and public life. As modern intellectuals such as Sigmund Freud and Karl Marx tried to show, demands for obedience to God and submission to religious authorities representing God (often male) have led to emotional repression, psychological exploitation, and social and economic oppression. Freud in particular argued that such religiously inspired claims come at too great a cost to the human psyche and civilization. The energy it takes to control one's behavior and emotions and the pathological symptoms it produces outweigh, he insisted, the solace and comfort brought by belief in an all-powerful Father God. Science, tentative in its claims to truth and open to correction, is far healthier and more benign than religion in understanding and responding to human suffering. Overemphasis on sin has damaged people.

A benevolent neglect of sin colors my own history. My denomination, the Christian Church (Disciples of Christ), certainly has streams within its tradition that have heeded what some have called the "dominant formula" of sin and salvation defining Western Christianity.[1] As one of the religious movements that emerged out of the fervor of the Second Great Awakening in the United States in the early 1800s, many Disciples still feature in their hymns and weekly communion the image of Christ's rescue from personal guilt that characterized the early camp meetings.

I did not grow up in one of these streams, however. The church I attended was shaped powerfully by another influence of the 1800s, the Scottish Enlightenment and its rational, pragmatic, empirical approach to faith. Faith entails reasonable affirmation of God and is demonstrated through action in the world designed to make it a better place for all people. The modern optimism about human nature of the mid-twentieth century just reinforced such leanings. Science and technology promised progress on all fronts.

Not surprisingly, neither my minister nor my Sunday school teachers nor my own parents spoke in any regular fashion about sin or the cross. As a rule, Disciples do not sing hymns in the minor key. We sing happier tunes. I can still picture the flip chart with the first hymn I learned by heart—"All Creatures of Our God and King"—filled with praise for God's creation and far removed from human wretchedness and the blood of Jesus. Confession and absolution of sin were neither part of regular corporate worship nor personal practice. This is true not only in my own home congregation but in many Disciples churches. Disciples have not made dispensing ashes on Ash Wednesday or marking repentance during Lent regular practices.

This approach to faith has positive aspects for which I'm thankful. I still have a rich sense of the presence of God in nature and often find my faith deepened by the woods, mountains, and seaside.

For the most part, I avoided punitive images of God and religiously sanctioned parental discipline in growing up. I gleaned the benefits of a church program focused on the life of Jesus—stories of his ministry healing the sick, praying in the wilderness, and urging care of neighbor and love of God. But, at the same time, I think I knew on some level that an important element of Christian thought and human life itself was missing.

Awakening to Sin

I can remember a day years ago by the lakeshore of a family summer camp when I first really *heard* the word *sin* in a way I had not before. Granted, it might have been spoken during my regular attendance in the church where I grew up, but the actual idea had not hit home. Sharing a swing set with a couple of other eight- and nine-year-old girls, I listened as one of them said something about confessing her sins. She apparently had to do this regularly. Her depiction did not enlighten me. She seemed equally amazed that the word was new to me and that I had escaped this practice.

It dawned on me then that I had missed something essential in the tradition and needed to know more about it. I had inadvertently stumbled upon a rather pivotal Christian theme. There was, I discovered in that early religious conversation, a word and way to talk about betrayal of self, others, and God, an experience of faithlessness to which I was awakening. In short, the word, despite all its shortcomings, provides a way to talk about an experience of brokenness to which most people awaken.

The demise of heavy sin language and all the guilt and shame that it carried has not been a wholly bad phenomenon. Yet this leaves completely aside a big question: How are Christians supposed to understand sin and salvation in the aftermath of Freud and his modern friends? Even more important for each of us, how can we understand the human anguish contained in the word *sin* if we cannot talk about it or have no word for it?

Tough theological words like sin, for all their trouble, open up new worlds. A member in my home church once teased me about all the words he had to look up, like "salvific," in a book I'd written. Initially, I felt apologetic. After all, this book was supposed to be for a wider public. Yet this church member is a physician. I know he uses loads of words his patients do not understand. Why is medicine allowed special language but not theology? Is it due to the public perception of religious faith as a private emotional confession rather than a lively, challenging intellectual enterprise? I gained a key insight from bumbling through my first religion course in college, a really tough class on a major philosopher and his slim volume on religion: When one learns fresh language, one can think about matters previously unfathomable. I had to create a glossary of terms I had seldom heard or used before—omnipresence, omnipotence, transcendence, immanence, and so forth—at the back of our assigned book, which I mistakenly thought would be easy because it was short.

Sin then is something to fathom, even if we think we automatically understand what it means. Even those traditional theological concepts that have caused so much travail at the level of Christian life and pastoral care have potential to enlighten and liberate. In a word, terms like sin help us see reality and human experience more fully.

I have not desired, however, the kind of comprehensive overview typically provided by systematic or dogmatic theology. Instead, as a good pastoral theologian I have tripped over the theme of sin on my way toward more pressing existential concerns. From my first class and publication on death (and sin) until my most recent teaching and writing on children (and sin), questions about human failure have subtly percolated through my work on these other human concerns.[2]

In my studies I have found that pastoral, liberation, and feminist theologians have tended to bracket sin, particularly in relationship to death and children. Neither is a topic that people like to associate with sin. People have misused the threat of sin with the ill and the young to provoke a last-minute confession or justify harsh discipline. With death, the specter of eternal condemnation scared many sick and dying into confession and profession of Christ and often not toward genuine remorse. With children, doctrines of sin have been used over the past four centuries (and still today) to defend corporal punishment and coerce desired behavior.

Yet talking about sin in direct relationship to such concrete matters as death and children rather than as academic abstractions might also hold liberating potential. My effort to do so in this chapter and in my work in general has led me from *sin* to the term *frailty* as an awkward and limited synonym for sin. Frailty is, of course, not the same as sin. But it operates as a key precipitant, a major component part, and a word that recognizes the complex experience of guilt *and* innocence, the experience best encapsulated by Martin Luther himself—*simil justus et peccator*, "at the same time righteous and sinner."

Sin Vanquished from Death and Children

Both medicine and psychology have largely taken over the task of interpreting death and children. Neither likes sin or frailty. In medicine, illness and dying are matters to be fought against and, when possible, conquered. Fueled by the remarkable twentieth-century progress made in isolating germs, discovering vaccines, and curing disease, people believed the modern myth that all illness can be eliminated, at least up until cancers, heart disease, and AIDS raised their ugly heads. Medical definitions of death as the cessation of mechanical body function or as a failure of technology make it hard to see death as a change in the status of the soul. Illness and dying seem more like value-neutral and even impersonal happenings than significant moral or spiritual events affected by sin and salvation. If they have such meanings, these are often considered subjective, private, and superfluous.

The renowned psychoanalyst Elizabeth Kübler-Ross became popular in the 1960s and 1970s precisely because she challenged such modern attempts to clean up and hide death.[3] But she did not do much to advance moral and religious understandings. In fact, like many psychoanalysts, she was deeply suspicious of institutional religion. She was especially critical of Christian portraits of death as the enemy over which God triumphs and of ministerial attempts to elicit confession from the dying. Death, she asserted, is a natural part of life, as natural as birth, and her five stages prize peaceful reception of life's end. Moving through shock to denial to anger to bargaining to the final ideal of acceptance depends on full emotional catharsis. Caregivers should elicit such emotional expression and never judge or impose their own values, she insisted. If guilt is discussed at all (sin never is), it is with the purpose of ventilating and working through it. Nearly a half-century later, people still name the five stages as a mantra for managing all kinds of frailty and loss. The stages do not include, it is important to note, any mention of confession, repentance, absolution, forgiveness, or reconciliation, at least not in such formal religious terms. Most definitions of a good death in modern medicine and psychology avoid any talk about judgment. This is a serious oversight.

A similar dynamic has arisen around children. It seems particularly backward to suggest that children are sinful, especially in light of the harmful consequences of this view in some conservative contexts. During the Enlightenment, people began to raise good questions about the perception of children as depraved. Philosophers such as John Locke and Jean-Jacques Rousseau argued that children are by nature social and affectionate, not sinful. However, despite the good intentions and positive repercussions of this new view, the contention that children are morally neutral, even fundamentally innocent, contributed to a growing romanticizing of childhood, perhaps most evident in Impressionist portraits and modern advertisements that endow children with almost celestial goodness. Viewing children through such rose-tinted glasses truncated and distorted their nature, knowledge, and capacities as full human beings.

Once again psychology served as a handmaiden. Alice Miller, once a psychoanalyst, has as much notoriety for her work on the dangers of narcissistic parents in the 1980s as Kübler-Ross gained through her work on death in the 1970s. To her credit, Miller falls into a long line of twentieth-century psychologists from Freud to clinicians such as D.W. Winnicott and Robert Coles who took children seriously when most systematic theologians had dropped them as a legitimate subject. As Miller powerfully testifies, adults must respect the full range of children's emotional needs rather than force them to gratify adult desires. Failure to do so results in an iniquity visited on later generations, as emotionally deprived children become parents who use their children to get the affirmation lacking in their own childhoods. Over time, however, Miller became more strident, more disenchanted with both psychoanalysis and Christianity, and she shifted her focus from emotional to physical abuse, eventually accusing Christians of perpetuating a "poisonous pedagogy" of cruel mental and physical techniques designed to render children obedient. Others, such as historian Philip Greven, have found ample evidence to argue that such discipline can indeed be quite hazardous to children's health.

Fresh awareness of the misuse and abuse of children has helped to improve their lot. However, most post-Freudian psychology has promoted a largely one-sided optimistic view of children and their inherently benevolent nature and a largely negative view of parents and society. When children fail to thrive, it regularly pictures them as victims of parental or societal pathology. Miller, for example, sees childhood mistreatment as the root cause of "*every* kind" of psychic disorder.[4] A child, she naively declares, "who has been allowed to be egoistic, greedy, and asocial long enough will develop spontaneous pleasure in sharing and giving."[5] Children, in other words, do not do wrong unless wrong is done to them. They develop altruism naturally, Miller believes. Parents need only stand back and watch. As with Kübler-Ross' assumption that death is completely natural, this is a huge religious and philosophical assumption that theologians and philosophers have debated for centuries. Do we develop altruism naturally? Many people would not agree. But how do we talk about sin and children?

In short, modern medicine and psychology dodge and occlude religion when it comes to the nebulous dynamic of sin, failure, and frailty. The last decade has seen a flurry of discussion about moral responsibility for health and an explosion of interest in spirituality. But most people still avoid the word *sin*. Sin is for the religious specialist.

Sin Retrieved

Shunning sin is a moral problem because it brackets major questions about human responsibility. But ignoring sin is also a spiritual and pastoral problem because it dissuades us from considering the use (and misuse) of our own vocational gifts and suggests a refusal to face deeper questions about life's meaning and our relationship with others and the divine. Yet how do we draw sin back into the picture of the dying and the child without perpetuating the harm done in sin's name?

Sin may sound old-fashioned and barbaric to modern ears, as neo-orthodox theologian Paul Tillich observes, but however we name it, we must acknowledge that in the end, in the face of human finitude, we are all "beaten by the consequences of our own failures." Sin does not refer here to a list of specific transgressions but to the more profound and disturbing act of "turning away from participation in the divine Ground from which we come . . . [and] the turning toward ourselves." One hears Luther's portrait of sin hovering closely in the background here—*incuravatus in se*, "the self turned or curved in on itself." Few definitions of sin in the past twenty centuries have ultimately surpassed the Apostle Paul's eloquent words in the Letter to the Romans, however. To echo Paul and the confessional liturgy itself, "We always do things which we should not have done and do not things we should have done. . . . We are not what we essentially ought to be in a concrete situation."[6] Plainly said, we do not do the good we know (see Rom. 7:15-23).

Christianity's ambiguous heritage with regard to sin actually goes straight back to the first major church theologian, Augustine of Hippo, and his controversial legacy on sin and children. People have labeled his portrait of the sinful child, satiated yet jealous in seeing another infant at its mother's breast, as distorted and absurd. Yet this also reveals his close observation of children and his keen sensitivity to human temptation and foible.

Augustine understands sin as misdirected, humanly unquench-able desire, a distorted craving that evolves and deepens as an infant grows to be a child, adolescent, and adult. He drew on common understandings of antiquity that delineated six seven-year-long stages of increasing moral and spiritual accountability from infancy to old age, a schema that still has relevance today. If an egotistic insatiability characterizes infants, Augustine pro-poses, disobedience is the notable sin of the second stage in which children acquire language, perceive adult expectations, and learn the rules. In adolescence, elementary rebellion takes on an increasingly insidious form of deliberate malice, tellingly exempli-fied for Augustine himself in his own youthful foray with friends into a fruit garden. They stole pears, he reports in his powerful *Confessions*, prompted by nothing else than the sheer delight of doing something wrong.[7] This adolescent development surpasses the grasping desire of early children and even outright insub-ordination of later childhood. Stealing pears does not just test the limits of rules but finally crosses over and directly assails the boundaries of basic human decency.

We are still left with the complicated question of how such for-mal theological definition and description hold value for Christian life with either the dying or with children. What difference might these views make at the grassroots level?

In considering illness and dying, it helps to recognize how sin alters our experience. It adds an intensifying element to the reality of finitude and the fear of dying, what St. Paul called the "sting of death."[8] Kübler-Ross talks about the fear of dying. But, except for brief mention of "unfinished business" and ways to take care of it, she overlooks the additional burden of shame and guilt for aspects of life we can no longer change or correct in the face of finitude.

Remedying sin in the face of finitude is more complicated than finishing up pending business precisely because humans are not only biological creatures for whom death is a *friend* but also moral and spiritual beings situated at the juncture of nature and spirit and standing in relationship to the wider community. So death is also an *enemy* that goes against the grain of all we had hoped to become. The fear and pain of loss is heightened because we alone cannot bring about life's consummation in any satisfactory way. Try as we might, it is finally beyond our power. No knowledge or rehearsal of the five stages brings about a perfect end. In other words, we know at a certain level that our lives stand "under judgment" in Tillich's words.[9] Even if we no longer believe that the original sin of Adam and Eve actually altered our nature, "there is profound truth," asserts another neo-orthodox theologian Reinhold Niebuhr, "in the thought of death as the consequence of sin."[10]

On this score, Luther was never one to mince words or duck hard sayings. Christians "know that their death, together with all miseries of this life, is to be equated with God's wrath." For him, the terror of death is a direct result of our awareness of God's displeasure over our sins. We must war and battle with "an incensed God" if we want to protect our salvation.[11] Although Lutherans often avoid connecting their practice of regular confession of sin with this acute awareness of death, Luther suggests a close correspondence between sin and its confession and facing our finitude and mortality.

In other words, handling illness and dying well are more difficult than medicine and psychology presuppose. One cannot escape death's pathos simply by turning to ever-advancing medical technology or the psychological harmony of nature. There is, in the words of nineteenth-century theologian Søren Kierkegaard upon whom both Tillich and Niebuhr rely heavily, a "sickness unto death" or despair about the actions of our lives far worse than death itself. It is this sickness that the age-old Christian concept of sin tries to grasp and address.[12]

Medieval practices of the art of dying understood this and established powerful ways to embody it. A good death required a fairly common ritual that included expression of sorrow, pardon, absolution, and a turning toward God for grace and assistance, practices that have languished in the face of medical and psychological protocols. Ultimately, Tillich asserts, because humans experience the despair of guilt, there is "only one 'argument' against death: the forgiveness of sin and the victory over him who has the power of death."[13] This power cannot come solely from nature but must come from beyond it. That is, an adequate answer necessarily involves salvation or, as Niebuhr says, "divine completion of human incompleteness."[14] Caring for family, friends, and other people in the face of death then requires bringing the power of faith to bear on the entire human experience of illness and dying in all its messy, confusing, horrific reality, not to get around or past illness or death, but to get through it.[15]

There is also profound truth in the idea of sin in childhood and parenthood, despite its troubling misuse in the history of childrearing. Endearing images of inherently innocent and altruistic children make it almost impossible to take their moral and spiritual action seriously. Any fault in childhood lies outside children in narcissistic mothers, absent fathers, a materialist culture, or a corrupt Christianity. Although in each case criticism of parents, culture, and Christianity is apt, understanding children as moral and religious actors gets almost wholly lost. The ideology of innocence has allowed adults to picture children as passive, trivial, and available to adult objectification and exploitation. Children are seen as cute but less often as capable, intelligent, desiring individuals in their own right. Such simplistic definitions of children in terms of what adults are not—"not sexual, not vicious, not ugly, not conscious, not damaged" in the words of art historian Anne Higonnet—especially strands adolescents, as if they ought to metamorphose overnight from child to adult and spare adults the complicated reality of children's lives.[16]

Reintroducing the idea of sin suggests a less simple alternative. It helps us move beyond the unfortunate dichotomy between children as villains or victims. Children are neither wholly depraved nor wholly innocent. Contrary to the sentimentalized view, they have valuable and increasingly complicated moral and spiritual lives. They are as much about "difficulty, trouble, and tension," as they are about "celebration, admiration, and passionate attachment." The view of the *knowing child* confronts adults, says Higgonnet, with "many more challenges as well as many more pleasures than any idea of childhood has done before."[17] Capacity for sin develops gradually, incrementally, over time. Adults who care for children need better understandings of this dynamic within children and within themselves, including the recognition that adults possess greater power and knowledge and therefore increased responsibility and guilt.

There is not, in fact, a one-to-one correlation between Christian ideas of sin and harsh punishment. In other words, saying children are sinful does not inevitably lead to their punishment, even if this is how some Christians have mistakenly interpreted the tradition. Seeing children as fragile moral and spiritual creatures can also potentially enhance adult empathy and accountability. Adults can no longer discount children and their obligations to them by surrounding themselves with pictures of cuddly, unblemished, blissful

infants. Instead, adults must take the labor of protecting and raising children a great deal more seriously. Parents and the Christian
community are obligated by the view of children and sin to nurture
them in the faith.

Equally crucial, human error and imperfection is endemic to
good parenting. Care of children asks much of us, and there is
plenty of failure. What parent hasn't yelled rather than understood,
flailed rather than sustained patience, forced rather than invited,
and stumbled along in all the other ways adults infringe on the full
personhood of a child and damage right relationship with children?
Acknowledging this helps discourage the perpetual cultural myth of
the perfect parent. The prevalent push in psychology to figure out
why children turn out the way they do is paralleled by an obsession in
self-help literature and talk shows to perfect children and parenting.
Recognizing the utter reality of sin and failure just might help avert
this prominent temptation and renew appreciation for the value of
time-tested religious practices of self-examination, circumspection,
confession, repentance, forgiveness, reconciliation, and hope as absolutely essential to family life. Failures are not occasions for despair
or unrelenting guilt, shame, and punishment. They instead are cause
for deeper awakening, remorse, reparation, compassion, and forma-
tion. Recognizing sin in children and adults allows us to quit pursu-
ing perfection of children or parenting and more readily accept our
shortcomings and pursue amends and grace.

Sin Reconsidered from the Underside as Frailty

This does not tell the whole story, however. There is still a
fundamental problem with how major Christian theologians have
viewed sin. Augustine, Luther, Kierkegaard, Tillich, Niebuhr, and
many others like them usually presumed as their primary subject the
free man who has the will to choose and the power to execute and
enforce his choices. Sin looks quite different from the eyes of a child
or at the bedside of the sick.

Liberation theologians of all sorts have demonstrated in recent years that those who are marginalized and oppressed are more often sinned against than sinners themselves. Although "we are all capable of evil," says one theologian, "we have not all been, in the same way, equally responsible for it." Everyone has the same capacity but those people with less power "have not had the same *opportunities.*"[18] In other words, there is an importance difference between the sin of the powerful and that of less powerful. Christianity has given extraordinary attention to sin and insufficient attention to the suffering of the sinned against.

We are more aware now than ever before in Christian history that such distinctions are important. When we consider sin from the perspective of the sinned against or the underside, it looks different.[19] Viewed from the underside, sin is seen as the dehumanization of the "other" exemplified, for example, by Christianity's subordination of women as inferior or by the denigration of any group of people as less than fully human.[20]

Here sin is redefined as a corporate rather than individual reality or act. It involves the social, economic, and political exploitation of women or the poor or blacks.[21] Human hearts are "broken" or "damaged" or "wounded," in the words of Rita Nakashima Brock, by social forces such as racism or patriarchy rather than inherently "evil, willfully disobedient, and culpable."[22] A similar view of the "deeply wounded heart" of the sinned against also appears in the 1980s in a movement of Korean theology that grew out of grassroots work with the economically and socially disadvantaged. Theologians, such as Andrew Park, propose a new Korean term—*han*—for the experience of the downtrodden who have suffered at the hands of others and for the anger, bitterness, rage, resentment, helplessness, anguish, and lamentation that suffering has caused. This sentiment touches individuals and communities and is often passed along from generation to generation following severe social, political, and economic injustice and exploitation. The term *han* is seen as more fitting here than sin, which Park reserves for the willful acts of those who victimize others. "Sin is the volitional act of sinners (oppressors)," he contends, "han is the pain of the victim of sin."[23] Again Christian theology has focused obsessively on the former and almost wholly neglected the latter.

These definitions leave some unanswered questions, however. Do such distinctions between oppressed and oppressor create a troubling dichotomy? Do they overlook how easily the oppressed becomes oppressor? Do the oppressed ever commit sin? If so, how do we understand their fallibility? Do terms like *woundedness* suggest something inflicted on persons rather than done by them and hence subtly undermine moral and spiritual responsibility of the oppressed? It is hard to stress corporate responsibility without losing a sense of individual accountability. But if this is true, how might we preserve the power and agency of the oppressed to assert influence over others?

Theologians have struggled over these questions. On the one hand, in one of the most direct challenges to traditional Christian views of sin as excessive pride and self-promotion, we find Valerie Saiving trying to understand the sins of the oppressed—women and mothers who are not tempted toward pride but are tempted instead toward self loss or, in her telling litany, to "triviality, distractibility, and diffuseness; lack of an organizing center or focus; dependence on others for one's own self-definition . . . in short, underdevelopment or negation of her self."[24] But, on the other hand, four decades later, spokespersons such as Park have questioned whether women's low self-esteem and distractibility are actually sinful if "there is no act of volition" involved. "*Women's lack of an organizing center is not sin*," he says, "*but han.*"[25]

From one perspective, the oppressors commit sin and the oppressed experience han or harm. But is it always so clear-cut? Oppression and patriarchy deepen sin, but do they explain it exhaustively? Do the subjugated contribute, even if only in distorted and limited ways, to their own entrapment and to the demise of others? Sin and han overlap, Park admits, and even intermingle. The "oppressed can be oppressors," he says. But I believe that these two are far more entangled and intermixed than he suggests.

Perhaps the word *frailty* can provide an alternative means to grasp human failure. The word is not a completely satisfactory solution to the question of the relationship of sin, power, and volition but it points a way forward. In particular, frailty reconnects us to the physical and embodied nature of Christian life. Historically, Christianity has corrupted the connection between sin and bodies by reducing the meaning of sin's bodily location to a focus merely on sexual physicality and specific immoral acts (for example, sin is adultery or eating chocolate cake is sinful). But when we talk about someone as *frail* we think almost immediately of both ends of the life cycle, the aged and the infant.

Although we recognize the aging and the newborn as literally frail, isn't everyone? Only fear keeps us from admitting this. And it only takes illness or the recognition of the fragility of our own children to remind us. When we are sick, we are more prone to regressive behavior as we try to rally resources to deal with the emotional and spiritual onslaught of the illness. Wendy Lustbader, a social worker who has worked closely with the ill and dying, observes, "We have come to fear frailty more than death. . . . Frailty coupled with abandonment has become our most dire existential dread."[26] To acknowledge frailty is to acknowledge utter dependence on others and the contingency of all life and the infectious nature of sin. This is perhaps partly what Martin Luther or John Wesley meant when they equated sin and disease. In his Lecture on Romans, Luther in particular compared the tension between sin and salvation to the ill person who has received promise of cure from the doctor but is still both ill and healed, *simil justus et peccator*.

Frailty points to the precarious balance between helplessness and responsibility at the heart of Christian life. It is different than woundeness. We are born frail or at least with the potential for frailty; we are not wounded by others. Niebuhr and Tillich, following Kierkegaard, talk about anxiety. But they worry more about misuse of our freedom in our anxiety rather than the anxious mishandling of our frailty. They recognize that "man," anxious about his freedom, slides easily down the slippery slope of sin. So men with power are tempted to misuse it to control others, thinking too highly of themselves, disguising any sign of weakness, and demanding their own way through force and violence. In each of these examples, the problem about which Niebuhr and Tillich worry is the prideful misuse of freedom in the face of finitude. By contrast, when sin is viewed from the underside, we see that humans—oppressor and oppressed alike—struggle more over their vulnerability than their freedom. Freedom is less the crux of sin than frailty. Our frailty, not our freedom, makes sin unavoidable.

Frailty recognizes the unstable nature of sin for both the powerful and powerless. It acknowledges that the powerless—children in particular—are more often recipients of evil and wrongdoing than free actors, without entirely forsaking the human ability to choose, despite weakness and insecurity. Without a sense of this paradox, we stand in danger of blaming others for wrongs of our own. Frailty suggests the Augustinian (and Lutheran) idea that people are bound *and* free, oppressed *and* oppressor, as much victims of sin as culprits. Oppressive forces larger than ourselves entrap us. But we also, at some point, consent and commit to this. Given human frailty or weakness or vulnerability, children will go astray, adults will inevitably fail children, and the ill and the dying and those who grieve with and for them will recognize acutely all the ways they have failed life and life has failed them.

Sin—A Multivalent Term

Perhaps the most important conclusion of this meditation on sin is to avoid premature foreclosure on pondering the term. The

Christian tradition has been consumed by the desire to determine the single root of sin and tempted repeatedly toward monolithic interpretations.[27] Often those who have determined sin's root meaning have done so from positions of power. These definitions have served to reinforce this position and to intensify the self-hatred of the disempowered. But sin, like theology, is a multivalent term. It has many meanings—transgression against God's law, alienation from God, enslaving power, unbelief, idolatry, exploitation—that reveal different aspects of a related reality. Frailty is not essentially superior to other understandings. But it does emphasize vulnerability as a key aspect of human fallibility.

Nearly every Sunday when I join in saying the Lord's Prayer, I hear my husband utter *sins* while everyone else around me follows the worship bulletin and common custom and asks God to "forgive our *trespasses* as we forgive those who *trespass* against us." He declares sins firmly because he sees it as a more authentic translation of Jesus' intention and the tradition's overall emphasis. I still say trespasses. He may be historically correct. But there is also something about trespasses or even debts that has a concrete ring. I can picture these. I can recall moments when others have inappropriately invaded my space or violated my personhood (and vice versa). With debts I am drawn to consider the literal compensation I owe or am owed for what I have done or have had done to me. Each of these terms— *sin*, *trespass*, and *debt*—shifts the emphasis while not wholly losing a handle on a notion that forbids exhaustive definition.

We should keep our ears and eyes open for fresh portraits. In a passage of the much acclaimed book, *Gilead*, that traces the ruminations a dying pastor for his young son, the pastor refers to Jesus' invitation to "become as one of these little ones." This means, the pastor says, "you must be stripped of all the accretions of smugness and pretense and triviality."[28] There is a nice definition of sin, I thought, that crosses over oppressor and oppressed—*accretions of smugness and pretense and triviality.*

Practical theology differs from other kinds of theology because it seeks neither precision nor a completely cohesive or systematic or logical understanding of life. This willingness not only to tolerate messiness but also to endorse it is one of the distinctive contributions of practical theology to the wider enterprise of theological expression. When working with people and their many struggles, the illogic of poetry is often the better guide.[29] The poetry of the Lord's Prayer itself contains reciprocal, parallel examination of wrongs on all sides. The question in prayer, as in practical theology, is not just the conceptual meaning of the theological term but how we might live differently in light of sin, whether in raising children, caring for the dying, or considering our role as oppressed or oppressor.

For Reflection

1. Do you agree that it is not popular to talk about sin much anymore? Why or why not? What are your own experiences with the language of sin growing up? What are some of the ways in which you have talked about sin recently? What are some ways in which you have avoided the term? Do you think negative views of the damage such talk has done has contributed to a disinclination to talk about sin?

2. Have you thought about sin in relationship to children or illness and dying? Do you see children as sinful? In what ways? Do you agree that sin complicates illness and dying? In what ways?

3. Does one's context change how one sins or experiences sin? How has your own context shaped your relationship to sin?

4. In what ways is frailty a helpful alternative way to talk about sin? What other ways would you define sin?

5. How do you think worship shapes your understanding of sin?

4

Salvaging Sacrifice

Sacrifice has been a real "fishbone" in the throat of Christians, at least as troublesome for daily life as ambiguity and frailty.[1] As with Christian views of sin, the promotion of self-sacrifice has done more than its fair share of damage. Questions about the meaning of sacrifice in today's world abound, so much so in fact that *Time* magazine did a feature story on the atonement a few years ago. Throughout the ages, the misuse or distorted understanding of the terms *servanthood* and *sacrifice* have led to less-than-Christlike actions by those who profess to be the church. Studies of slavery and civil rights, for example, show how Christological images of servanthood have been employed to exploit people of color. Studies of abused children have found that a high number come from homes where Christian views of a punishing God and blood sacrifice are the staple. The sheer number of women who have died from domestic violence, all too often compelled to remain in dangerous situations by Christian mandates that women should submit to their husbands unquestioningly or endlessly sacrifice themselves for their family and church cannot help but make us sputter and choke. With this history, it is no wonder then that some people have begun to question Christianity's core belief in God's saving action as primarily one of substitutionary sacrifice. Everyday Christians—not only scholars—wonder about the obsession with self-sacrifice as a time-honored motif in Christian faith.

Yet, despite these concerns, powerful images of sacrifice live on in liturgy, film, and the lives of people. Sacrifice is built into the language of worship and the annual liturgical calendar (as I noticed acutely one spring when I passed a church sign that stated: "Lent—a time for self-sacrifice"). A few years ago, we saw the extent to which sacrificial imagery grips the heart of the American public when sacrifice hit the big screen in *The Passion of Christ*. All told, sacrifice is indeed, as one theological dictionary entry puts it, "one of the most inescapable, impenetrable, and off-putting themes in Christian thought."[2] For many, the Christian ideal of self-sacrifice, as interpreted by church tradition and promoted in society at large, misrepresents both the intent of God's creation and the promise of the gospel message itself.

So is there anything salvageable about sacrifice? The answer to this question is complicated. To love others in the midst of life's ambiguities and frailty, one needs some ability to sustain self-sacrifice. This has been a major oversight in popular culture and contemporary psychology and theology. But, at the same time, there is good reason for apprehension and avoidance. So, on the one hand, the category has been abandoned too hastily. But, on the other hand, if we want to salvage Christian views of sacrifice, we must begin by contesting the ways they have oppressed and harmed rather than saved and empowered.

Sacrifice as a Questionable Ideal

I have been thinking about sacrifice for a long time, maybe even before I realized it. Several years ago, when a systematic theologian asked me what made my thoughts on family and work theological, I evaded the question. In my book, *Also a Mother: Work and Family as Theological Dilemmas*, I did not talk explicitly or systematically about formal theological doctrines. But I can say now, looking back, that in a roundabout way (that is, in the way of practical theology), the book is actually about sacrifice or it is at least the initial germination of my own more extended struggle with the idea.[3] My own thoughts on the subject flow from the cry of women and mothers—myself and others—caught between the cultures of self-sacrifice and self-promotion, between the undying ideals of the "Father-Knows-Best" family of the 1950s and the sketchy ideals of working women. This has led to sometimes trivial, sometimes revelatory conflicts about what to do, how to live well, and how to spend one's time, often further complicated by poverty, abuse, racism, chronic illness, and other life-changing factors. No matter how women design their lives, most would admit that conflicts between self-interest and self-sacrifice plague their solutions to questions of work and love. As men assume more responsibility for home and children, this is increasingly true for them as well.

So what Christian value and disposition do I endorse if I uphold neither sacrifice nor its ready alternatives? Self-respect, mutuality, shared responsibility, interdependence, and justice all have merit, but the simple phrase just love, a phrase used by many other people, including my coauthor Herbert Anderson, is perhaps the best way to talk about what I mean. Just love does not rule out genuine acts of sacrifice and affection. It simply tries to make greater space in family love for the intentional pursuit of fairness and reciprocity in sharing the benefits and burdens.

Though I am still largely satisfied with this vision, two issues linger. First, Christian theology has changed dramatically for some of us, raising serious questions about the centrality of sacrifice in the Christian gospel, but worship, steeped in centuries of tradition, has not. Prayers mimic regularly sung hymns, depicting what Christ "hast suffered all for sinners' gain." Reliance on sacrificial imagery is particularly characteristic of non-liturgical traditions, such as my own, where elders make up their own communion prayers and often draw on the only image they know—sacrifice. But the motif is also powerfully embedded in high-church Eucharistic liturgies that proclaim the "Lamb who was slain, whose blood set us free." New Testament scholar Joanna Dewey notes that, "Virtually every time a Christian attends church the understanding of Christ's death as blood sacrifice and the corollary understanding that what is demanded of Christians is self-sacrifice are reinforced."[4] So, how does one deal with the cognitive dissonance in our spiritual lives between traditional views of the passion, as graphically filled theaters a few years ago, and recent protests about the cross as a harmful image? Is there something about our emotional and spiritual make-up that yearns for sacrificial imagery?

Second, questions about sacrifice emerge in daily life. Doesn't the sheer routine of home and work and human finitude itself still require one to postpone, if not forfeit or sacrifice, our own desires for the good of the other, whether the individual other or the corporate body of family and community? Sometimes my husband and I experience our entire shared life at home and work as one big round of sacrifice. Something propels me to extend myself for my children to a greater extent and at higher cost than I might have once thought possible. In fact, isn't this very impulse of love and protection for the frail and needy in one's own family precisely the impulse that Christianity has commanded us to extend to our neighbors at large? Does this kind of Christian sacrifice have any bearing in every day life any more?

Sacrifice under Siege

When did this impasse about the place of sacrifice in daily life begin to arise? Concern about women's self-sacrifice surfaced most powerfully in Christianity in the early 1960s and reached a climax in the 1980s. Almost five decades ago, women began questioning whether striving to sacrifice themselves for others was a fitting Christian mandate for women. In the years since then, many other people have added their voices to a growing theological stance that portrays the image of a Father God bent on sacrificing his son as condoning passivity before violence and perpetuating domestic abuse. These are serious charges, whether one agrees with them or not.[5] Questions raised by these charges about the place of sacrifice in daily life have largely gone unanswered, even though systematic theologians, including Lutheran theologians, have given renewed attention to formal doctrines of the cross.[6]

Criticism of Christian views of self-sacrificial love first arose directly out of the context of parenting, as women reconsidered its demands and questioned modern myths about innate maternal love. When it comes to parenting, selfless love may be a Christian corrective for men but it has often been detrimental to women. Time and again, people interpret the motivation behind maternal love of children, especially infants and children with high developmental needs or disabilities, as completely self-sacrificial and largely instinctive and natural. Once and for all, feminist theologians hoped to set the record straight and loosen the stranglehold of sacrificial love on ideals of Christian parenting.

The "most revealing lesson the children taught us," says Christine Gudorf, Catholic ethicist and mother of three children, two with severe disabilities, is that love can never be disinterested or entirely sacrificial. Although initially she and her husband gave considerably of themselves to a two-year-old who could not walk, talk, or eat and to a five-year-old who could barely walk, dress, or wash, selfless love was not a primary factor. Their giving was never unconditional or self-disregarding. Instead it involved a necessary give-and-take from the beginning. Self-interest actually enhanced their capacity to give. As this mother says, "the children were considered extensions of us, such that our efforts for them rebounded to our credit. Failure to provide for them would have discredited us. And we had expectations that the giving would become more mutual." If parents are honest, "every achievement of the child is both a source of pride and a freeing of the parent from responsibility," and not the result of a sacrificial urge.[7] Ultimately, even under the most difficult circumstances, her children enrich her life and give her hope, fresh loyalties, and a richly altered identity. Ten years later, Gudorf still insists that the sacrificial image of parenthood is a distortion that masks the real dynamics of love.[8]

Sacrificial love is not the right ideal to hang over the heads of women already over-programmed to give and give, leaving them ashamed of the self-interest that accompanies their love. Parents do better to admit and even affirm the needs they have for pleasure and gratification. When such needs are disguised as loving gifts for which others should feel grateful, such so-called sacrificial love can harm the recipient as well. Long-standing ideals of love exaggerate the amount of energy that a single person can or should bestow on children or household, misjudge the needed contributions of other adults, deprive men of opportunities to learn the labor of attentive love, and deny the raw ambiguity of maternal love (that is, that a mother can both love her kids and detest caregiving). Myths about maternal devotion convey the message that women are innately gifted and men somehow ill-equipped to share child rearing and housekeeping.

Self-sacrifice and Beliefs about Christ

What does all this talk of parenting and children have to do with theology? We are not just talking about good housekeeping here. The distorted view of what children and parents owe each other is intricately connected to bad Christology or to Christian understanding of the meaning of Christ's life and death. The portrait of maternal love as heroic self-sacrifice results not just from a major misunderstanding of parenting and personal relationships in general, but also from a misunderstanding of Jesus. As Gudorf puts it, "Jesus did not come to earth to give himself disinterestedly to save us. Jesus was motivated by a mutual love with 'Abba'" and "felt impelled not only to love others, but to bring others into the relationship he shared with 'Abba.'" Although Jesus did urge sacrificial action, he did not pursue sacrifice as a good unto itself. He connected the demand for sacrifice with the promise of a mutually beneficial reward in the kingdom to come of which the present rewards of mutual love are already a partial taste. Moments of self-diminishment, even the moment of sacrifice on the cross, are, she says, "just that—moments in a process designed to end in mutual love."[9]

Other theologians extended this argument even further and ruled out sacrifice completely, ultimately declaring, as Protestant ethicist Beverly Harrison did, "Mark the point well: *We are not called to practice the virtue of sacrifice.*"[10] Society has consistently undervalued women's ability to bear and nurture life. We need to appreciate women's capacity to nurse the other into being. This does not mean, however, a return to sacrificial womanhood. "That we have turned sacrifice into a moral virtue has deeply confused the Christian moral tradition," says Harrison. Christians have taken the crucifixion out of its historical context and turned sacrifice into an abstract norm. Jesus did not seek death as an end in itself. He faced it as result of his refusal to abandon his more radical vision of love, that is, solidarity with those on the margins of his community. Jesus "*accepted* sacrifice," as Harrison argues, but only "*for* the cause of radical love, to make relationship and to sustain it, and, above all, to *righting* wrong relationship."[11] Sacrifice may be the consequence but it is not the highest calling of the Christian life. Radical acts of solidarity and reciprocity are the key virtues.

Maternal Sacrifice as a Daily Practice

Twentieth-century theological ethicists have argued at length about whether *caritas*, a Latin term for love that is often associated with mutuality, is more fundamental to the Christian message than unconditional sacrifice, often equated with love as *agape*. Some trace our negative view of self-love right back to Martin Luther. For Luther, love of others precludes self-love. He defined sin, after all, as *incuravatus in se*, or the self turned or curved in on itself, as we saw earlier. According to Lutheran theologian and churchman Anders Nygren, Luther saw self-interest as "vicious" and contrary to true Christian love of neighbor, which "has the task of completely dispossessing and annihilating self-love."[12] The tradition prior to Luther did not exclude self-love so rigorously. Patristic and medieval theologians portray *eros* (sexual love and desire) and mutuality as viable components of Christian love.

In focusing so extensively on this conceptual or theoretical debate about *eros*, *caritas*, and *agape*, however, theologians often give Luther too much blame and credit. Certainly Luther formulated a Christian ethic that opposes self-love to love of others. But modern ideas about self-sacrifice and the atonement were shaped as much by material realities of family life over the last century and a half as they were by doctrinal debate.

The Victorian era in the nineteenth century sacrilized, privatized, feminized, and whitewashed sacrificial domesticity as a virtue for white, middle-class mothers in particular. Congregational pastors and theologians created powerful new understandings of the family's religious role. The home became a private refuge with the sacrificial love of mother for child at its emotional center. One prominent spokesman at this time, for example, compared God's love to that of a mother's exhaustive love for her child. The mother, he says, "takes every chance for sacrifice for it as her own opportunity. She creates, in fact, imaginary ills for it, because she has not opportunities enough of sacrifice."[13] Another well-known clergyman claimed that "the love most like God's is an 'unselfish' love 'that makes suffering itself most sweet, and sorrow pleasure,'" a love best exemplified by mothers, who are by nature "unselfish and long-suffering."[14] No wonder many of us experience the rejection of a sacrificial Christianity as an assault on God and our own mothers.

Both then and now, Christian claims about God are powerfully shaped by the daily practices of family life. Challenging the nature of a mother's sacrificial love for her children is partly threatening because it means questioning how we understand God's love. Everyday family life shapes our doctrines of love and the cross, more than we often realize.

Sacrifice and Child Abuse

For many people, it is ultimately the problem of child abuse, not the dilemma of parenting, that reveals the deepest problems with sacrificial images of God's love. Theologians who have viewed Christian claims about Christ's sacrifice on the cross through the eyes of children with abusive parents have raised the most acute questions. They accuse the traditional doctrine of sacrificial atonement of upholding the abuse of the Son by God the Father or of promoting what they christen as "cosmic child abuse" in which the "father allows, or even inflicts, the death of his only perfect son." Such doctrines, one theologian says, "are a result of the abusive treatment of children in a patriarchal culture." Genuine salvation comes not through sacrifice but through intimacy. Genuine love requires self-awareness and self-affirmation and not egoless self-sacrifice.[15]

This has led many people to a drastic conclusion. Formally recognized doctrines of atonement—ransom, satisfaction, and moral influence—are all seen as bankrupt. They are all marred by a harmful and destructive glorification of suffering, sacrifice, and death. Suffering has no redeeming value. "We must do away with the atonement," they argue, "this idea of a blood sin upon the whole human race which can be washed away only by the blood of the lamb." For them, the cross is purely a political event. Jesus died an unnecessary, violent death because he challenged the unjust systems of his time.[16] This leads inevitably to a deeply troubling question with which others have had to contend: Is anything left of Christianity if we throw out the atonement?[17]

Salvaging Sacrifice

This discussion leaves sacrifice shipwrecked and for good reason. Sacrifice has hung over the heads of many people, distorting rather than edifying the good news of abundant life. Is anything salvageable? Is it possible to resurrect anything from the wreckage if destructive understandings are still alive and well in contemporary culture?

Webster's Dictionary defines *salvage* as the "act of saving or rescuing property" in danger of destruction by a calamity, such as a wreck or fire. I happened upon the word partly because of alliteration (*salvaging sacrifice*). But it fits. The debate does concern the church's property. Sacrifice is a piece of intellectual and ritual capital that has long defined the church. *Salvage* also fits because it implies a moderate path forward. The property has some value, despite all the damage, but the entire piece itself is not worth saving. Moreover, reentering the site of calamity involves some risk. I tread on, aware of the hazards. Three areas—family, community (including global community), and spiritual life—call for rescue efforts. I want to look briefly at each of these before concluding with an outline of the limits and parameters of such retrieval.

As we will see, salvage is not just a matter of revitalizing a tattered and lost asset. It transforms and redefines the recovered good. Sacrifice still means giving oneself for the good of another without assurance of a return gift. But it must now occur within a wider context of supporting structures that either alleviate the loss and destruction that accompany such self-giving or justify its necessity. Guided by this definition, sacrifice actually comes closer to exemplifying the original meaning of the Latin word *sacrificium* from which it is derived: "to make holy" or "to sanctify" (*facere*, "to make"; *sacer*, "holy").

Rescue Efforts

Despite all the problems with the term, sustaining family life requires daily self-restriction, whether we call it sacrifice or not. The ability of adults to care for others and to become creative, procreative, and productive persons requires sacrifice in all kinds of families—heterosexual, gay, lesbian, single, blended, nuclear, intergenerational, extended, and so forth. Psychologists who have written about adult development and theologians who have talked about adult fulfillment often overlook this. An acquired capacity to sustain sacrifice is especially important, though not solely so, in relationship with children. Those theologians and psychologists who have espoused radical mutuality have often done so in an adult-centric, chronological void, assuming equal adults as the subjects and ignoring children, the aging, and those at different stages of non-equal dependency. Failure to include the routine realities of raising children has resulted in a lack of understanding of the necessity of transitional sacrifice or the temporary restriction of our own demands and desires for the sake of our children.[18]

On a fairly regular basis, care of children calls for a kind of self-denial and sacrifice of ego gratification that is not often found outside the family, insists pastoral theologian Brita Gill-Austern, motivated partly by her experience raising three kids. "No relationship can exist in a perpetual state of perfect mutuality," she asserts.[19] As both Herbert and I have argued, parents alter their lives to live according to the pace of children.[20] One may get a great deal back, but the return is seldom instantaneous or in kind. Realistically, the very difference between children and adults who care for them makes it difficult, if not impossible, for the moments of sacrifice to balance out, even in the long run.

Sacrifice has relevance not only in parent-child relationships but also between parents in relationship to children. Without some place for sacrifice, the pursuit of radical mutuality between two parents responsible for childcare and housekeeping easily degenerates into a parsimonious tit-for-tat computation of the exactingly fair distribution of domestic labor. Recognizing sacrifice as transitional and sometimes necessary might allow one to suspend such calculations and to care without as much begrudging the cost. The term makes particular sense for men who have seldom been socialized to give up their own interests for the sake of childcare and housework. Men who hope to assume a fair share of domestic responsibility need to know more about self-sacrifice than experts in the women's movement and advocates of mutuality ever anticipated.

Sacrifice is also relevant in the wider context of work, community, and global society. Many people perpetuate a false and unfortunate dichotomy between the home as a site of sacrifice and the workplace as a site of self-fulfillment. This is not always the case. Many working class women and women of color, for example, have worked because they needed to secure the welfare of their extended families and not because they sought individual growth. Many jobs, particularly menial and low-paying jobs, do not guarantee personal satisfaction. They often require sacrifice of time with family. Even in fulfilling jobs, there is still the necessity of subordinating one's own good to the good of others. Helping professions in particular, like teaching, ministry, social work, and so forth, often require moments and more extended vocational or life-cycle phases in which one's individual aspirations take a back seat and one works for some other institutional good beside one's own advancement.

The notion of sacrifice seems especially important in our current cultural and political context but in a different way than the Christian right commonly presumes. Conservative Christians endorse renewed marital commitment, issuing a call of sacrifice for the family. But all too often this becomes a "moral veneer," as Catholic ethicist Lisa Cahill says, for the promotion of a particular family structure and the good of one's own kin, class, and ethnic group. Christian sacrifice should have another meaning entirely. Narrow family values of responsibility and fidelity must be combined with altruistic social action, including the willingness to sacrifice to meet the needs of others *beyond* the biological family. *The* Christian family is not, in Cahill's words, "the nuclear family focused inward on the welfare of its own members but the socially transformative family that seeks to make the Christian moral ideal of love of neighbor part of the common good."[21]

Sacrifice also has an important place globally, although once again in quite a different way than in the current conservative wartime political rhetoric of heroic sacrifice of young soldiers dying for their country. What might it mean within our global context of unjust distribution of goods between developing and more developed countries to lay down power and relinquish control over a portion of the world's overall wealth?[22] In our current climate of instant gratification, conspicuous consumption, imperialistic politics, and global warming, this kind of extension of Christian sacrifice seems warranted.

Finally, the concept and practice of sacrifice still has a place in spiritual life and worship. The desire for atonement corresponds directly to our awareness of our own human frailty and the depth and extent of failure, shame, and guilt from which people stand in need of relief. Granted, some of this shame and guilt is neurotic and unwarranted, as modern psychology has demonstrated. But some is warranted. Falling short of our hopes and burdened by transgressions too heavy to carry, people hunger for someone to "bear our griefs" and "carry our sorrows" in the words of Handel's "Messiah" and Isaiah (53:4). People seek an image of God, as Herbert Anderson notes, who "stops at nothing to redeem us" and "who not only suffers with us but sacrifices for us"—sacrificing not a victimized son but God's own self.[23] Jesus' life, death, and resurrection grant moral and spiritual release. Such imagery and the liturgical acts that embody release serve a deep-seated emotional and spiritual need for reprieve from frailty. They provide compensation and cleansing, accomplishing that which we cannot do for ourselves. The emphasis on God's sacrificial action in Christ speaks to this need for relief, unmerited love, and grace.

Limits and Parameters in Salvaging Sacrifice

There are, nonetheless, some absolutely essential parameters to this activity of salvage. Any act of rescue must recognize that the property will never be the same again, as I have noted. Moreover, the entire property itself is not worth salvaging.

We must carefully heed the criticism of the past two decades. This means listening to those harmed, acknowledging the dangers and abuse of the imagery of sacrifice, and avoiding oversimplification (either seeing sacrifice as the only way to interpret Jesus' death or ruling atonement out of the Christian life completely). Gill-Austern's project of reclaiming sacrifice, for example, comes only after she traces the economic and political inequities and distorted emotional and spiritual reasons, including atonement theology, that lead women to sacrifice themselves inordinately and destructively. We must listen carefully for the distortions of glorification, subordination, and victimization.

If self-giving has an essential role to play in sustaining family, spiritual, and political life, a key question becomes how to distinguish life-giving from unhealthy, life-denying forms.[24] In other words, there are standards by which we can measure sacrifice's legitimacy. Theological ethicist Barbara Andolsen, for example, specifies three occasions in which sacrifice is justifiable: when practiced by the privileged on behalf of the oppressed, when a party in greater need has a *prima facie* claim on others, and when occasions of sacrifice can be balanced out over the long run.[25] As a basic rule, self-sacrifice is legitimate when understood within a larger life-cycle perspective that is attentive to the fluctuations of mutuality and sacrifice that surround relationships of dependency.[26]

Ultimately, to discern the difference between exploitative and salvageable sacrifice, feminist theologians have made clear that we must ask a series of complex questions pertaining to the motivation and aim of sacrifice and the nature of the person's selfhood. Is the sacrifice and surrender chosen and invited rather than forced or demanded? Is it motivated by fear or genuine love and faithfulness? Does the person remain a subject or is she turned into an object and a means to someone else's end? Does the sacrificial loss actually count as gain in some deeper way and enrich rather than destroy life?[27] Does sacrifice, in essence, remain subordinate to and in the service of more abundant life and does it lead to more just and loving relationships?

In short, self-sacrifice must rest on the bedrock of self-regard, respect, and mutual reliance. It must involve agency or the ability to make the choice to act for others. Such love actually entails "not *self-lessness* but self-fullness," as Catherine Keller suggests.[28] Theological ethicist Daniel Bell makes this point well:

> The recovery of sacrifice hinges on revisioning it not in terms of scarcity, where giving necessarily entails losing, but in terms of abundance, wherein giving is a matter of sharing an inexhaustible surplus. In other words, the recovery of sacrifice entails seeing it as a central practice in a cycle of gift-exchange, in which giving does not result in loss but rather nurtures communion, mutuality, and interdependence.[29]

This kind of self-sacrifice differs from the self-denial proclaimed by traditional Christianity *and* the self-loss critiqued by feminist theology.

Using Language of Sacrifice with Care

In the end, the term *sacrifice* itself must be used with greater attention and care. We often do not think consciously about the language we use and take for granted in congregational worship. We do not usually ask ourselves, for example, whether a prayer was appropriate or the anthem worked well with the sermon. To enter fully into worship, it is often necessary to calm temporarily that part of our active minds that analyzes, measures, and judges. But church leaders, whether elders who pray or those who preach, must help Christians think harder about the cross and communion table. Contrary to common understanding in congregations, the cross has never had one singular meaning but rather a whole host of conflicting interpretations, all of which have some bearing on the celebration of the Eucharist. The view of Christ's death as a sacrifice is by no means the sole or even the dominant New Testament explanation. In fact, the idea that Christ died for our sins is significantly absent from early Christian sources. Sacrificial theories of the atonement were not "fully articulated until the eleventh century" and never made mandatory by any major church tradition. One of the "odd features of the Christian tradition" is "that, while the notion *that* Christ saves lies at its heart, the church has never developed an official position on just *how* that salvation is accomplished."[30] Although we have formal doctrines about Christ's nature and the nature of the trinity, for example, we have no such doctrine about the cross. In other words, Christians should know that salvation has many meanings, not just the one that has dominated Western Christianity of Christ's death as a vicarious sacrifice for our sins.

What then are alternative understandings? Everyday Christians need an atonement primer or a rudimentary tutorial on classic and contemporary readings. There are several theories besides the *satisfaction theory*, which arose in medieval and reformation theology and dominates current popular Christianity in the United States with its view of Christ's death as satisfying a debt owed to God that saves us from sin. The *ransom theory*, going back to patristic theology, understands Christ's death as paying a price owed to the devil that saves us from evil. *Moral influence theory*, suggested in the eleventh-century writings of Peter Abelard and linked with modern liberal theology, interprets Christ's death as an inspiring instance and example of love and obedience that reconciles us to God. Contemporary *liberation theory* sees Christ's death as an unjust consequence of radical action on behalf of the oppressed, a sign of resistance to injustice that heralds the kingdom of God. Other contemporary theologians protest even the latter and portray the cross more bluntly as the evil use of violence by the powerful, literally an instrument of public execution and, as such, neither redemptive nor liberative.

This complexity and multiplicity in the tradition must be more adequately explained and represented in prayers, hymns, and sermons than has been the case. Even the words, "the Lamb of God who takes away the sin of the world," need not mean that one is offering up Jesus to appease God. Rather these words may indicate, as Anderson says, that humanity "demands a victim and the suffering God ... in Jesus dies at the hands of the victimizers."[31] Although we must take great care not to idealize and romanticize suffering, Luther's theology of the cross reminds us that God is powerfully present in suffering.

The meaning of the cross depends on where one stands on the continuum between oppressor and oppressed, sinner and sinned against. The cross promises forgiveness for the former and empowerment for the latter. For the sinned against, the cross may not invite confession, justification by faith, and forgiveness as much as constructive anger, compassionate confrontation, challenge to unjust structures, and redemptive liberation. Reformation theologian John Calvin himself understood this. "If the death of Christ be our redemption," Calvin declared, "then we were captives; if it be satisfaction, we were debtors; if it be atonement, we were guilty; if it be cleansing, we were unclean."[32] To encompass fully the complexity of suffering and God's compassion, a plurality of images and models are needed.

Self-Sacrifice in Everyday Life

There is still a place for sacrifice but not without serious awareness of the damage it has wrought and not as the sole understanding of the cross at communion. Just as the sin of pride is not the only or even the primary human quandary addressed by the Christian story, neither is forgiveness of sin the only meaning of salvation. God's saving action in Christ also answers questions of human vulnerability, disempowerment, abandonment, injustice, hatred, exclusion, discrimination, betrayal, negation, loss, lament, and death. Jesus' dying as a divine protest against injustice, as witness to God's power over evil, and as an embodiment of divine participation in death and the triumph of new life have as much importance as Jesus' dying to atone for our sins.

This examination of sacrifice reveals how deeply Christian doctrine emerges out of and remains embedded within the dynamics of common life, especially family and worship life. The dynamics of family—who loves whom and in what way and, in particular, the sharp gender polarization between men and women—has had a powerful influence on formal Christian doctrine and devotional life. To make changes in family life (such as, share care of children) or in congregational life (redo the hymnal, for example) involves us immediately in the thicket of Christian doctrine. For some, questions about doctrines of atonement arise in direct response to dire circumstances of brutality and violence. For others, including myself, the question about sacrifice flows from more mundane circumstances.

Regardless of the conditions that provoke doctrine, all of us face the difficult question of how to go on living faithfully in households and congregations that are now more aware than a few decades ago of the almost insurmountable flaws in religious tradition and its misuse by the cultural elites at the expense of the disempowered. Rather than the usual theological questions of whether Christian doctrine is true or coherent, we face new questions today about whether Christianity will help or hinder our living. Since Christian claims about sacrifice have the capacity to both oppress and liberate, the spiritual practice of discerning theological wisdom in the midst of daily life, so central to the discipline of practical theology, becomes absolutely essential.

For Reflection

1. What kind of damage have theological claims about self-sacrifice caused in your own life? If you do not think they have done any damage in your own context, can you understand how people in other contexts might feel differently?

2. Are there places and situations where you believe language of self-sacrifice seems appropriate and necessary? How would you access the various kinds of sacrifice in your own life right now?

3. When your congregation partakes of the bread and wine during Eucharist, are these basic elements imbued with a variety of meanings? How are these meanings conveyed? How do these meanings become embodied in your own life?

4. How should our country's citizens change their behavior and dispositions in light of Christian claims about sacrifice in relationship to the wider world context?

5

Witnessing Wonder

The birth of a child is a moment that evokes wonder. We are astounded by an infant's delicate hands, tiny toes, and loud noises. There is a fierce dignity of the newly born that sometimes startles us. In an essay on Mary, mother of Jesus, Bonnie Miller-McLemore makes this observation about her sons: "If I attend to my three sons, daily I am astonished and dazed—by spontaneous humorous comments, by their sheer persistence in the face of daunting challenges, by shoes larger or shoulders taller than mine, or by small acts of gratitude and love returned to me unasked for and unexpected."[1] Awe is intrinsic to good parenting, she says. It is a dependable sign of parental love when parents list their children first among those in whose presence they have felt wonder or awe. Wonder is a necessary virtue that affects how we practice faith's wisdom at home.

Wonder and awe are also attitudes of the soul crucial for human survival on a shrinking planet. In order to hold this disposition of wonder toward whomever or whatever is different, we need to suspend judgment, be willing to be surprised, and allow our world to be expanded to include more difference. If there is a piety in cultural anthropology, "it is the conviction that astonishment deserves to be a universal emotion."[2] The same is true for Christian piety. We bear witness to daily occasions for wonder because we believe the mysteries of God are hidden in the ordinary.

Psychiatrist Alfred Margulies proposes that wonder is an essential aspect of understanding "the other" because it promotes "a searching attitude of simultaneously knowing and not-knowing, of finding pattern and breaking apart, that goes against the grain of our organizing mind."[3] In order to celebrate diversity and be hospitable toward difference, we need to be receptive to ambiguity and regard "the other" with wonder. When we understand with eyes of wonder, we are open to new meaning because we look beyond the patterns of previous knowledge.

Wonder mixes astonishment with curiosity toward the unexpected or the inexplicable. Wonder promotes an awareness of transcendence in everyday living that trumps every human effort to demystify life. Wonder diminishes the misuse or abuse of people by inviting respect for the worth of each person. Wonder fosters an appreciation for "the other"—whether the other is the homeless person we pass on the way to work or the turbaned Sikh neighbor riding his lawn mower or the child in our midst or God.

Distinguishing Wonder and Awe

We frequently use wonder and awe interchangeably though they have slightly different meanings. While wonder is our response to a pleasant surprise, awe includes our awareness that surprise may be unpleasant. When wonder includes awe, we know that the unexpected may evoke terror. In *Apology for Wonder*, written thirty-five years ago, Sam Keen connected wonder with ambiguity. Because we fear the unknown as deeply as we dislike paradox, we will seek to minimize the unexpected and the unexplained. According to Keen, "When we are wonderstruck our certainties dissolve, and we are precipitated suddenly into contingency."[4] And if contingency makes us anxious or afraid, we will ignore wonder in order to avoid awareness of contingency and frailty.

Borrowing from the work of Rudolf Otto, Sam Keen makes a connection between wonder and the experience of the Holy that helps us understand awe. "In *The Idea of the Holy*, Rudolph Otto showed that the holy is always experienced as at once *tremendum* and *fascinans*—awful, fearful, threateningly powerful, and at the same time fascinating, desirable, promising, and compelling. Wonder partakes in this same ambiguity."[5] We are simultaneously frightened and affirmed, vulnerable and secure. However difficult it is to hold this paradox, we know all too clearly that the mystery of God and the mystery of life evoke both wonder and awe mixed with both fear and terror.

Our experience of God in the ordinary moments of life may be *mysterium tremendum* as well as *fascinans*. We are fearful of our creatureliness and our insignificance and our vulnerability in the presence of very real threats from both human activity and the natural world. Global acts of terrorism, tsunami-producing earthquakes, hurricanes that devour cities–all evoke new dread. The biblical mandate to show hospitality to the stranger seems unrealistic and even naïve in the face of homeland insecurity. Neighbors we have known for years suddenly become dangerous because of their religion or their origins. In this time of terror, wonder turns toward awe, mixing fascination and terror and becomes more problematic and yet, paradoxically, even more essential.

The trivialization of wonder and awe is one of the causalities of modern technological living. We use "wow" to advertise new computer products. "Shock and awe" is a high-tech military strategy designed to bring an enemy to its knees. One might hope that the frequent use of "wow" or "awesome" in casual conversation is an inarticulate recognition of the extraordinary wonder and mystery of life. However, "wow" seems to have little to do with wonder, as it is generally understood. Instead, "wow" is an ambiguous response appropriate for an age of uncertainty that is partly about shock, partly about curiosity, and a little about not knowing what to say. It is less skeptical than "no kidding." It is the kind of thing one might say on a boring date or in the middle of a boring conversation. The casual use of "wow" can dilute our sense of wonder or domesticate awe so that we miss seeing traces of mystery in the ordinary.

The Ordinary Oddity of Things

Welcoming diversity and seeing traces of transcendence in the ordinary of life are more likely to occur when wonder is a disposition of the soul. Moreover, we are more likely to endure moments of terrifying awe if we have been attending all along to daily wonder. Practicing being attentive to ordinary awe is preparation for those inevitable times when an unsettling or terrifying experience shatters the safety of our world or our understanding of what it means to be human or the orderliness of our theology or the predictability of our visions of God. Practicing attentiveness to wonder in ordinary moments is prelude to respect for "the others" whom we inevitably meet in our pluralistic world. Witnessing wonder fosters attentiveness to the transcendence of God before whom we live.

Two lines in the "Prayer of the Elephant" from *Prayers from the Ark* by Carmen Bernos de Gasztold provide us with an image for reflecting on ordinary occasions for awe and wonder. "Give me such philosophic thoughts, that I can rejoice everywhere I go in the lovable oddity of things."[6] Ordinary awe is seeing fresh snow sparkling with diamonds in the light of night. The song of a bird as morning dawns, fall leaves blowing in the trees, the lover's grace that takes our breath away, the smell of grass in the morning dew, unexpected gestures of kindness from a stranger, the extravagance of God's coloring of nature in the spring and in the fall, the sounds of grandma's laughter in the evening shadows all invite us to rejoice in the lovely oddity of things. In those moments, we respond with wonder and astonishment at the hidden mystery of God.

Some years ago, an elderly parishioner described how easy it is to overlook everyday occasions of wonder and awe:

One morning, I was sitting at my kitchen table, staring into space. It was one of those windy days when the sun keeps coming in and going out. All of a sudden, a sunbeam crossed my kitchen table and lit up my crystal saltshaker. There were all kinds of colors and sparkles. It was one of the most beautiful sights I'd ever seen. But you know, that very same saltshaker had been on that table for fifty years. Surely there must have been other mornings when the sun crossed the table like that, but I was just too busy getting things done to see it. I wondered how much else I'd missed. This was it; this was grace. I needed crippled hands before I could sit still. Sometimes you have to be stopped right there in your tracks before you can see that all of the beauty of life is right in front of you.

Ordinary awe is an invitation to a dance of images and ideas, of knowing and not knowing, of wonder and reason through which we glimpse traces of the majesty and wonder of God in everyday experience.

After his father's death, David Miller wrote a moving tribute about him in *The Lutheran* magazine:

> For who knows what beauty and love lies waiting to be received among the broken pieces of a life you didn't choose? God surprises. Grace is real and unpredictable. Incomprehensible mercy haunts our days. There is always more—more life, more beauty, more hope, more wonder, more joy, more than we think or imagine. Such is the courage of small things—and its faith.[7]

When we witness wonder in the ordinary, we see remarkable truth in the broken and mundane. In faith, we see the unexpected and strange as a theatre of divine grace. Wonder is a disposition of the soul that welcomes surprise and invites respect for difference. Astonishment is a Christian virtue in the face of mystery. What are the theological resources that will strengthen the witness to wonder in daily living?

The Ordinary, the Incarnation of Our Lord, and Wonder

The belief that the ordinary carries the wonder and grandeur of God is a central motif in Lutheran theology and a particular theme in Luther's Christmas sermons. Incarnational theology is a resource from faith's wisdom that encourages us to see the ordinary with wonder and awe. Luther's question about the birth of Jesus, according to Roland H. Bainton, "was not whether God could or would make a special star, but why the Lord of all the universe would care enough about us mortals to take our flesh and share our woes. The condescension of God was the great wonder." [8] This is the mystery that reason cannot fathom.

The condescension of God was the great wonder. So we stand with shepherds and Mary before infant with tiny toes and milky burps, and we are awed by an awareness that God loves the ordinary. If we fail to pay attention to the ordinary, we may not see God hidden in the Infant of Bethlehem. Luther describes the pure wonder of the birth of Jesus this way:

> Our God begins with angels and ends with shepherds. Why does he do such a preposterous thing? He puts a Babe in a crib. Our common sense revolts and says, "Could not God have saved the world another way?" . . . God does not even send an angel to take the devil by the nose. He sends, as it were, an earthworm lying in weakness, helpless, without his mother and he suffers him to be nailed to a cross. [9]

There is no escaping the creatureliness of Jesus who paradoxically carries the majesty of God hidden as an "earthworm lying in weakness." From his birth, Jesus is like every human creature who is paradoxically from the earth and from God.

Luther says it best of all in a sermon on the Presentation of our Lord as he reflects on Simeon's blessing:

His wonders no reason can comprehend. Wonderful is it that in the midst of death is life, in the midst of folly there is wisdom. Let us, then, take heart. How wonderful that the Child of a poor abandoned maid should become King of the World! It does not make sense. Wonder brings faith. He who does not believe cannot understand, know, or see. He who understands cannot but wonder.[10]

Wonder brings faith. Wonder and awe are not impediments to faith but in fact the prelude to faith and faithful living. Wonder and awe are dispositions of the soul for faith and for daily living in a world teeming with splendid diversity. If we fail to pay attention to ordinary difference, we may not see God hidden in the world. The paradox of incarnational theology is that God is revealed in hiding.

This passionate proclamation of God's love for the ordinary is mirrored in the Lutheran approach to worship. In *Holy Things*, theologian Gordon Lathrop reminds us that when we gather in the Christian assembly we "start with the simple things, the common human materials, then see how communal meaning occurs as these things are juxtaposed to each other and gathered together with speech about the promise of God. In this way, the assembly and the materials it uses become a rich locus of meaning, *casting light on all common life.*[10] As with paradox, Lutheran theology of wonder has been honored better in theory than practice. "Casting light on all common life" is an underutilized emphasis of Lutheran incarnational theology. In this time when religious and cultural diversity are as near as our families, astonishment and awe need to be a pervasive and permanent part of the soul's desire as we connect the wisdom of Luther's theology for Christian practice in daily living.

Overwhelmed by Awesome Life Moments

You may have said on occasion, "I have too much on my plate," or "It's all a little too much!" You may have decided not to watch the news because there is too much irrational suffering in the world. As we noted in chapter 2, we often are willing to trade treasured freedoms for safe absolutes when we are overwhelmed with ambiguity and uncertainty. When we are overwhelmed by too much difference in our lives, we make all strangers dangerous and retreat into gated communities to make the world smaller and safe. When too much irrational suffering in the world overwhelms us, we may turn from life to avoid the pain. When we fear the unexpected, we try to domesticate strangeness to feel secure. If we have become less open to surprise, however, we may miss seeing signs of the wonder of God in our ordinary days. In that sense, being overwhelmed may be an impediment to wonder.

If we feel overwhelmed, it is not necessarily because we are weak or lacking courage to cope with all the complexities of modern living. We may feel overwhelmed simply because life has become more porous. Because we can witness bodies falling and buildings crumbling and dead children floating down stream on cable news while we eat breakfast, suffering anywhere in the world becomes our own. Stress from anywhere in the world is more likely to penetrate inside our private space. Moreover, we are susceptible to being wounded by the air we breathe, the water we drink, the mail we receive, the sun that shines, and maybe even the people with whom we make love. We are vulnerable, and likely to become more so, as the contexts in which we live become more diverse and more porous. We also are more readily overwhelmed because we have not developed the cognitive skills demanded for living with ambiguity, uncertainty, and diversity.

David F. Ford, Regis Professor of Divinity in Cambridge, England, has proposed "multiple overwhelmings, both good and bad" as *the* metaphor for living in these days. According to Ford, the basic question is, "how, in the midst of all our overwhelmings, are our lives shaped?"[11] It is not just terror that overwhelms us. The world's suffering that invades our lives from every corner of the globe also overwhelms. The particular plight of committed and compassionate people is that suffering anywhere in the world reminds us of what we have not done. The intrusion of the unseen faces of the suffering ones is enough for most conscientious people who feel overwhelmed. In order to cope with "multiple overwhelmings," we need to name our emotion ("I am overwhelmed"), describe what is happening, and then expand our ways of imagining the world to include being overwhelmed. That is not unlike acknowledging that vulnerability is part of being human. Learning to see the ordinary as an occasion for awe, whether fascinating and terrifying, forms an attitude of the soul that prepares us for those times when we will face multiple situations that overwhelm us.

When we feel overwhelmed, we tend to protect ourselves from the awareness of suffering and pain. We will cover the soul with protective armor, fashion compromises, and drift into indifference in ways that prevent us from living fully. We flee from life in order to flee from fragility and death or "multiple overwhelmings." In order not to flee from life, we need to acknowledge our own fragility and vulnerability. Through awe we come to know how overwhelming life is and how readily our presumptions crumble. It is also through awe that we are awakened to the majesty of life and the mystery of God. Both are true. We need the wisdom that awe inspires. At the same time, the awe that leads to wisdom is rooted in the paradoxical view of the human creature as wondrous and frail. Witnessing wonder in the ordinary, including full sensitivity to ordinary struggles of separation and loss and disappointment and anxiety of daily living, will help to fashion souls hardy enough for faithful living in these times.

If the soul's disposition of wonder is shaped by the cross of Christ, we know we cannot flee from the world's suffering without fleeing from a suffering God. The cross is a sign that to be in the presence of suffering is to be in the presence of God. We are being formed by being overwhelmed as we live under the shadow of the cross. Breathing deeply enough to absorb the world's pain, seeing suffering with a compassionate heart, embracing as much of the anxiety and ambiguity of life as we can—all invite us to practice living with an awareness of "multiple overwhelmings." It is living the Jesus way.

Near the end of *Lament for a Son*, author Nicholas Wolterstorff writes these words about his grief: "I shall try to keep the wound from healing, in recognition of our living still in the old order of things. I shall try to keep it from healing, in solidarity with those who sit beside me on humanity's mourning bench."[13] The God who inspires wonder in nature and the ordinary of daily living is also known to us in the suffering of the cross. We will discover the mystery of the suffering God as we sit "on humanity's mourning bench" or when we do not ignore our children's anxiety or when we do not flee from being overwhelmed by our neighbor's anguish. The way to live without becoming completely overwhelmed is to allow ourselves to be overwhelmed everyday as we live with contingency and pain and suffering and yet believe the promise that God is present in the struggle. We stand in awe and proclaim the good news that God suffers with us as well as for us.

Dispositions of the Soul that Will Strengthen Wonder

We have suggested, following from the work of Amy Plantinga Pauw, that desires and dispositions tutored by the Spirit of Christ play a key role in connecting beliefs and practices. Embracing ambiguity is the missing link between the paradox perspective in Lutheran theology and a gracious response to difference in a pluralistic age. Wonder is the soul's motivating inclination that invites us to see and bear witness to the mystery of God and "the other" in ordinary encounters of living. Because the soul is often overwhelmed by too much diversity and suffering or too little certainty and security, wonder does not stand alone. Four related dispositions will buttress the soul's sturdiness for faithful living: humility, the willingness to struggle, the capacity to be moved, and gratitude.

The first disposition is humility. Wonder presumes humility. When humility is a disposition of the soul, we will be less arrogant and more respectful toward whomever we regard as "other." A few years ago, a 700-pound, saucer-shaped probe landed on Saturn's moon after a journey of seven years. The idea that there is something seven years away from where I live is astonishing and humbling. It is humbling to be aware of how little we are. When we understand how small we are in the vast scheme of things, we are less likely to be puffed up with false importance. When we feel little, we are glad to remember that we are held in the loving care of God. Humility is a prelude to wonder.

Humility is a human feeling, and it is more than a human feeling; it is the way of God with us. Never overpowering, never controlling, only leading gently from love, Jesus reverses human notions of victory, success, and dominance and rejects all forms of arrogance. Jesus is the humble one who embodies the humility of God. Humility is therefore the Christian way with one another. "Let the same mind be in you that was in Christ Jesus, who . . . emptied himself . . . being born in human likeness. And being found in human form, he humbled himself and became obedient to the point of death—even death on a cross" (Philippians 2:5-8). This humility is more like self-forgetfulness than self-modesty. Such humility aims at partnership, not domination, at faithfulness, not success by the world's standards. Humility as self-forgetfulness makes it easier to honor difference and celebrate the gifts that diversity brings. Forgetting ourselves on purpose is a way to practice wonder. It is a reminder that it is not all about us.

The second disposition is the willingness to struggle. The vulnerability and frailty of human folk is reason enough to add the willingness to struggle as a disposition of the soul. Our frailty, because it comes with being creatures, is one of God's gifts. Just as ambiguity paradoxically leads to clarity, so vulnerability leads to strength. And the more we embrace ambiguity and diversity and uncertainty, the more we understand faithful living as struggle. When we add to the mix a particular Lutheran sensitivity to human frailty and sin, then struggle has yet a deeper dimension.

When we are signed with the cross in baptism, we are initiated into a life of struggle. *Simul justus et peccator* is the Lutheran way of formulating the ongoing struggle against forces, seen and unseen, that would eliminate awe before the mystery of God's gracious love. *Simul justus et peccator* is, on the one side, a guard against the threat of despair from our persistent struggle with human sin, and, on the other side, a guard against the danger of false security in God's grace because of our persistent desire to flee from struggle. It is easier to see the wonders of living with God when we expect struggle.

The third disposition is the capacity to be moved or changed. Awe-based faith begins with the capacity to be moved. The previous chapter explored the inescapable need for communal beings to sacrifice for the sake of others. Loving others, without holding back anything, begins with the willingness to be changed by the needs of others. The willingness to be moved by another's story or another's thought reduces conflict in marriage, introduces compassion into every human interaction, and builds a fence around domination or colonialism of any form. At the micro level, marriages are more likely to endure when husbands are able to acknowledge that they have been influenced by their wives. At a macro level, there is mutuality of influence between the local and the global. Modern globalization, wherever it occurs and whatever its origins, is a process that curves back on itself and reshapes the local.

Jesus exemplified the compassion of God when he responded to the desperate plight of those who came to him. Compassion describes our capacity to be moved by the pain of another. To show compassion is to cry out with those in misery, to mourn with those who mourn, to weep with those in tears – to have their pain on our hearts. We should expect to be changed by these empathic encounters with others if only that our understanding of what it means to be human is enlarged by the stories we hear. We are sustained for this ministry of compassion by our willingness to be moved by the extraordinary gifts of others, the unexpected kindness by a friend, the picture of a city draped in fog, the laughter of a child as well as the loving mystery of God. We are changed by wonder; and openness to being changed makes wonder possible.

Gratitude is the fourth disposition of the soul. Gratitude is both attitude and action. It is included under the soul's desire because the attitude of gratitude comes before acting gratefully. In his book *Before God*, George Stroup has observed that "to live before God means that human beings, along with the rest of creation, are called to live gratefully and in everlasting praise of God, that is, to live doxologically."[14] Nick Canaday, a member of a parish I served as pastor, had been raised Christian Scientist. As he was dying, Nick struggled with a fear that he had no faith. He had beliefs and he held them passionately. He had loved God with all his mind but it was the discovery of gratitude that made it possible for Nick to love God with his heart as well. For Nick, gratitude was the beginning of a faith of the heart. "I will be forever grateful" became the preface to every remembrance in his life.

Living gratefully and doxologically is at the heart of the practice of the Christian life. We are always giving thanks, not as we ought, but as we are able because we have been overwhelmed by the extravagant grace of a generous God. Because all is grace, entitlement has no place in the Christian life. Because all is grace, we begin every adventure by giving thanks for the mercies of God and the gift of life. Because all is grace, we live with an enduring awareness that we do not possess our life, but have it as gift. Gratitude is the essence of Christian practice and the human counterpart to the grace of

God. *If we begin whatever we do with gratitude, we will see the gifts of God in life with eyes full of wonder and awe.* Wonder and gratitude are inseparable.

In a culture of exchange and merit, we need to find new ways to speak about grace and gratitude. Human beings often are described exclusively in terms of their capacities and limits. Our worth is measured by what we make happen. It is a worldview of works without grace, of performance without promise. At the end of the movie, *Saving Private Ryan*, the captain sent to save Private Ryan is dying. He looks at the unharmed private and says, "Earn this! Earn it." With that, the movie flashes forward to Ryan as an old man. At the end of his life, at the end of the movie, Ryan asks his wife if he was a good husband. He is fearful that he had not met the qualifications of earning his own life back. The Christian gospel is a counter word to this culture of merit. We are free to live fearlessly before God and before one another because of God's saving love. It is a gift that can only be received with deep gratitude and awe. Before God, everything is wonder. And wonder and awe in daily life take the form of gratitude for all things.

Transforming Practices

Practical theology reflects carefully on Christian practices in daily living in the light of particular theological traditions. Our approach to practical theology has included an emphasis on the motivating implications of the soul that connect beliefs with practices in the Christian life. Embracing ambiguity, we have suggested, is an inner disposition informed by a Lutheran paradoxical perspective that will enable us to live in a time of uncertainty by saying the other side in personal and pastoral situations. Wonder, the soul's desire that is necessary for this time of pluralism and terror, is sustained by witnessing to the wonder of God in the ordinary. Seeing with eyes of wonder makes us attentive to signs of transcendence and the outrageous love of God in daily activities. Wonder is a prelude to faith. We will be more likely to practice awe in the ordinary if humility, compassion, and gratitude are added to wonder as dispositions of the soul.

Still, we must ask the question with which we began this book one more time. What is the connection between what we believe and how we live? Do we regard the Christian faith as a source of wisdom for daily living? What practices in daily living, enriched through eyes of awe and wonder, will embody incarnational theology? If we start with encounters in daily living, how will seeing the wonder of God in the ordinary cast a gracious light of God on common life? The following four practices illustrate how daily living is transformed by embodying wonder and awe.

1. The practice of "empathic listening" is a consequence of seeing others through eyes of wonder. By empathy I mean the capacity to understand the world of another and imagine that world as it is understood by the other and then convey that understanding in speech and action in such a way that the other feels heard and understood. Empathy begins by setting aside the clutter of our lives and respecting the uniqueness of another. It requires careful listening and accurate responding to what has been heard and not said. Empathy demands that we nurture the ability to hold in tension differing and even contradictory worldviews without needing to judge or make rational recommendations. The aim of empathy is to build human bonds, transcend difference, foster recognition, and demonstrate genuine acceptance of the other person. In a world teeming with diversity, we would do well to begin by practicing empathy as often as we can.

2. The practice of "ecumenical gift exchange" embodies wonder toward the gifts that strangers bring to communities of faith. Whenever someone joins a congregation from another denomination, we invite them to identify the gifts they bring from that faith perspective. Diversity is a common treasure. We may discover along the way that differences complement rather than contradict. In ecumenical gift exchange, the gift giving enriches all the participants, since we do not lose our gifts when we share them with others. Theologian Margaret O'Gara makes this point: "The gift exchange of ecumenical dialogue is the discovery that some of the differences among Christians that were once thought to be contradictory are now recognized as complementary."[15] Similarly, in order to insure that we are thinking about baptism in relation to the one, holy, catholic church, it has been suggested that someone from another denomination be visibly present at a baptism to embody the unity of the church in the act of Baptism.

3. "Appreciative Inquiry" is a method of organizational conversation and planning that invites conversation about the world we most desire. Appreciative Inquiry provides a different way for people of an organization to discover the deepest knowledge and highest future of that system at moments of wonder. "At its core, Appreciative Inquiry is an invitation for members of a system to enhance the generative capacity of dialogue and to attend to the ways that our conversations, particularly our metaphors and stories, facilitate action that support members' highest values and potential."[16] While the focus of appreciative inquiry is on organizational life, it is a perspective that could enhance every human interaction. Beginning with wonder toward one another helps create an environment in which all gifts are honored and in which a new future is fashioned from the questions we ask of the present and the past.

4. Wonder toward "the other" is the soul's disposition that enables the practice of hospitality toward the stranger as an embodiment of the gracious and inclusive love of God. The Japanese theologian Kosuke Koyama has said that, "the only way to stop the violence of genocide in our world is by extending hospitality to strangers."[17] Showing hospitality is not only the essence of the gospel; it is necessary for survival in an increasingly pluralistic world. Being formed in the practice of hospitality is also critical for our time because it invites us to explore different ways of thinking about what is public and what is private. Roman Catholic lay theologian Rosemary L. Haughton proposes that home is a place of encounter between the public and private and hospitality is how home functions. Here is how she describes her paradoxical vision: "I use the word *hospitality* in a wide sense that expresses the willingness to make common, at least temporarily, what is in some sense private, which is how we think of home.[18] The family is the primary context in which we learn how to practice this art of hospitality.

Concluding Words

In the beginning, we suggested that every practicing Christian is a practical theologian. By that we mean something quite simple and quite complex. Every Christian, to live faithfully in a pluralistic context with multiple, competing views of reality, must be able to sustain a coherent and consistent connection between beliefs and practice. The gap that often exists between faith and practice is bridged by greater attention to the dispositions of the soul. The soul's desires or dispositions connect faith's wisdom with the practices that our context of uncertainty and pluralism call forth. In the end, we need to be able to practice theology by heart, without notes, from the heart.

Faith is more than doing; it is being in the world as a sign of the presence of God. God's love of the ordinary in the Incarnation is our invitation to see the world through eyes of wonder. If we see with eyes of wonder, we will be thrilled to see traces of God in the unrecognizable stranger or the homeless women or the child in our midst. At the same time, moments of awe may terrify and overwhelm. Our encounters with divine mystery occur between yes and no, fate and freedom, faith and doubt, strength and weakness, or any of the contraries of daily living. It takes courage to embrace ambiguity without looking for certainty in the wrong places.

Wonder, as another disposition of the soul, also increases our ability to live in the midst of diversity. If we see with wonder and practice awe in the ordinary, we are more likely to suspend

premature judgments and allow our world to be expanded to
include the rich diversity of God's creation. Wonder opens the soul
for surprise, adventure, and deeper dimensions of meaning. In that
sense, before God and before one another, wonder is both an end
and a beginning.

For Reflection

1. In your daily round of activities, what ordinary instances of wonder and awe grab your attention and what or whom do you easily
   overlook? What changes do you need to make in your pattern of
   living in order to see clearly signs of the mystery of God in the
   ordinary?

2. Is the frequent use of "wow" or "awesome" in casual conversation
   simply a manner of speech or is it an acknowledgment that life is
   full of mystery? How do you regard the use of "wow" in advertis-
   ing new technologies or other commercial ventures?

3. Wonder is very much a part of a child's experience of immediacy.
   What reasons do we use to explain why it is a disposition that we
   need to outgrow as we move toward adulthood?

4. How is our openness to wonder affected by fear? What does the
   widespread presence of fear mean for Luther's statement that,
   "wonder brings faith"? Are there instances in your life when you
   have experienced fascination and terror simultaneously?

Notes

Chapter 1

1. Niels Henrik Gregersen, *The Gift of Grace: The Future of Lutheran Theology* (Minneapolis: Fortress Press, 2005), 4,13, 16.

2. See Kathryn Tanner, *Theories of Culture: A New Agenda for Theology* (Minneapolis: Augsburg Fortress, 1997), 71-92.

3. S. H. Blank, "Wisdom," in *The Interpreter's Dictionary of the Bible: An Illustrated Encyclopedia* (Nashville: Abingdon, 1962), 857.

Chapter 2

1. Michael Moynahan, SJ, "Litany of Contradictory Things" in *Orphaned Wisdom* (Mahwah: Paulist, 1990), 104-106.

2. Pat Parker, "For the White Person who Wants to Know How to Be My Friend," in *Movement in Black: The Collected Poetry of Pat Parker, 1961-1978* (Ann Arbor: Firebrand, 1990), 99.

3. Ernest Becker, *The Denial of Death* (New York: Free, 1973), 26.

4. Paul Tillich, *The Courage to Be* (New Haven: Yale University Press, 1952), 148. Italics added for emphasis.

5. Tillich, *The Courage to Be*, 149. Italics added for emphasis.

6. Cynthia D. Moe-Lobeda, *Public Church: For the Life of the World* (Minneapolis: Augsburg Fortress, 2004), 2.

7. Sylvia Dunstan, "Christus Paradox," (Chicago: GIA, 1990).

8. Parker J. Palmer, *The Promise of Paradox: A Celebration of Contradictions in the Christian Life* (Notre Dame: Ave Maria, 1980), 38.

9. Palmer, *The Promise of Paradox*, 46.

10. Niels Henrik Gregersen, Bo Holm, Ted Peters, and Peter Widmann, *The Gift of Grace: The Future of Lutheran Theology* (Minneapolis: Fortress Press, 2005), 4.

11. Amy Plantiga Pauw in *Practicing Theology*, ed. Miroslav Volf and Dorothy C. Bass (Grand Rapids: Eerdmans, 2002), 34.

12. Pauw, *Practicing Theology*, 47.

13. See Gordon W. Lathrop, *Holy Things: A Liturgical Theology* (Minneapolis: Fortress Press, 1993).

14. James Fowler, *The Stages of Faith* (San Francisco: Harper & Row, 1981), 198.

15. Paradox is a central motif of a series of books on family life cycle written by Herbert Anderson with others and published by Westminster John Knox, Louisville. *Leaving Home* (1993); *Becoming Married* (1993); *Regarding Children* (1994); *Promising Again* (1995); *Living Alone* (1997).

16. H. Newton Malony, *Living with Paradox: Religious Leadership and the Genius of Double Vision* (San Francisco: Jossey-Bass, 1998), 7.

Chapter 3

1. Wanda Warren Berry, "Images of Sin and Salvation in Feminist Theology," *Anglican Theological Review* 60 (January 1978):26.

2. *Death, Sin and the Moral Life: Contemporary Cultural Interpretations of Death* (Atlanta: Scholars, 1988); and *Let the Children Come: Reimagining Childhood from a Christian Perspective* (San Francisco: Jossey-Bass, 2003).

3. Elisabeth Kübler-Ross, *On Death and Dying* (New York: Macmillan, 1969) and *Death: The Final Stage of Growth* (Englewood Cliffs: Prentice Hall, 1975).

4. Alice Miller, *The Drama of the Gifted Child: The Search for the True Self*, completely revised and updated, trans. Ruth Ward (New York: Basic, 1994), 10, emphasis in text.

5. Alice Miller, *The Drama of the Gifted Child: How Narcissistic Parents Form and Deform the Emotional Lives of their Talented Children*, trans. Ruth Ward (New York: Basic, 1981), viii.

6. Paul Tillich, *The Shaking of the Foundations* (New York: Charles Scribner's Sons, 1948), 19; *The Eternal Now* (New York: Charles Scribner's Sons, 1956), 52, 56; and *The Meaning of Health: Essays in Existentialism, Psychoanalysis, and Religion*, ed. Perry Lefevre (Chicago: Exploration, 1984), 234.

7. Augustine, *Confessions 2.4*, trans. Henry Chadwick (New York: Oxford University Press, 1991), 28-29.

8. Paul Tillich, *The Courage to Be* (New Haven: Yale University Press, 1952), 17.

9. Tillich, *The Meaning of Health*, 190.

10. Reinhold Niebuhr, *Principles of Christian Theology* (New York: Charles Scribner's Sons, 1966), cited by Roy Branson, "Is Acceptance a Denial of Death?" *The Christian Century* (May 7, 1974): 466.

11. Martin Luther, *Luther's Works*, vol. 13, Selected Psalms II, ed. Jaroslav Pelikan (St. Louis: Concordia, 1956), 112.

12. Søren Kierkegaard, *The Sickness Unto Death*, trans. Walter Lowrie (Princeton: Princeton University Press, 1941), 146, 150-54, 195.

13. Tillich, *Shaking of the Foundations*, 172.

14. Reinhold Niebuhr, *The Nature and Destiny of Man: A Christian Interpretation*, 2 vols. (New York: Charles Scribner's Sons, 1941-1943), vol. 2, 287-88.

15. Thomas Lynch, "Good Grief: An Undertaker's Reflections," *The Christian Century* 120, no. 15 (July 26, 2003):22.

16. Anne Higonnet, *Pictures of Innocence: The History and Crisis of Ideal Childhood* (New York: Thames and Hudson, 1998), 224.

17. Higonnet, *Pictures of Innocence*, 209.

18. Rosemary Radford Ruether, *Sexism and God-Talk: Toward a Feminist Theology* (Boston: Beacon, 1983), 180-81, emphasis in text.

19. Andrew Sung Park and Susan L. Nelson, eds., *The Other Side of Sin: Woundedness from the Perspective of the Sinned-Against* (Albany: SUNY Press, 2001).

20. Ruether, *Sexism and God-Talk,* 20, 163, 180-81.

21. Gustavo Gutiérrez, *A Theology of Liberation: History, Politics, and Salvation,* trans. and ed. Sister Caridad Inda and John Eagleson (Maryknoll: Orbis, 1973), 25-37 and James Cone, *A Black Theology of Liberation* (Maryknoll: Orbis, 1990), 107-108 cited by Park and Nelson, *The Other Side of Sin,* 11-12, 23.

22. Rita Nakaskima Brock, *Journeys by Heart: A Christology of Erotic Power* (New York: Crossroads, 1988), 7. See also her chapter, "And a Little Child will Lead Us: Christology and Child Abuse," in Joanne Carlson Brown and Carole R. Bohn, eds., *Christianity, Patriarchy, and Abuse: A Feminist Critic* (New York: Pilgrim, 1989), 55.

23. Andrew Sung Park, *The Wounded Heart of God: The Asian Concept of Han and the Christian Doctrine of Sin* (Nashville: Abingdon, 1993), 10, 12.

24. Valerie Saiving (Goldstein), "The Human Situation: A Feminine View," *Journal of Religion* (April 1960): 108.

25. Park, *The Wounded Heart of God,* 12, emphasis in text.

26. Wendy Lustbader, "Thoughts on the Meaning of Frailty," *Generations* (Winter 1999-2000): 1.

27. Berry, "Images of Sin and Salvation in Feminist Theology," 47.

28. Marilynne Robinson, *Gilead* (New York: Farrar, Straus, and Giroux, 2004), 30.

29. See Bonnie J. Miller-McLemore, "The Subject and Practice of Pastoral Theology as a Practical Theological Discipline," in Denise Ackermann and Riet Bons-Storm, eds., *Liberating Faith Practices: Feminist Practical Theology in Context* (Leuven, Belgium: Peeters, 1998), 175-98.

Chapter 4

1. My image of the fishbone comes from Daphne Hampson, ed., *Swallowing a Fishbone: Feminist Theologians Debate Christianity* (London: SPCK, 1996).

2. Ian Bradley, "Sacrifice," *The Oxford Companion to Christian Thought,* ed. Adrian Hastings, Alistair Mason and Hugh Pyper (Oxford: Oxford University Press, 2000), 637. See also his book, *The Power of Sacrifice* (London: Darton, Longman, Todd, 1995), 1.

3. Bonnie J. Miller-McLemore, *Also a Mother: Work and Family as Theological Dilemma* (Nashville: Abingdon, 1994).

4. Joanna Dewey, "Sacrifice No More," *Distant Voices Drawing Near: Essays in Honor of Antoinette Clark Wire,* ed. Holly E. Hearon (Collegeville: Liturgical, 2004), 160.

5. The next four sections trace selected highlights of the debate about Christian self-sacrifice. Readers interested in specific scholars and publications will find names and sources in the notes.

6. See, for example, Mary M. Solberg, *Compelling Knowledge: A Feminist Proposal for an Epistemology of the Cross* (Albany: SUNY Press, 1997) and Deanna A. Thompson, *Crossing the Divide: Luther, Feminism and the Cross* (Minneapolis: Fortress Press, 2004).

7. Christine E. Gudorf, "Parenting, Mutual Love, and Sacrifice," *Women's Consciousness and Women's Conscience: A Reader in Feminist Ethics,* ed. Barbara

92   Faith's Wisdom for Daily Living

Hilkert Andolsen, Christine E. Gudorf, and Mary D. Pellauer (San Francisco: Harper & Row, 1985), 181-183.

8. Christine E. Gudorf, "Sacrificial and Parental Spiritualities," *Religion, Feminism, and the Family*, ed. Anne Carr and Mary Stewart Van Leeuwen (Louisville: Westminster John Knox, 1996), 300-301.

9. Gudorf, "Parenting, Mutual Love, and Sacrifice," 176, 185-86.

10. Beverly Wildung Harrison, "The Power of Anger in the Work of Love: Christian Ethics for Women and Other Strangers," *Making the Connections: Essays in Feminist Social Ethics*, ed. Carol S. Robb (Boston: Beacon, 1985), 19, emphasis in text.

11. Harrison, "The Power of Anger," 18-19, emphasis in text.

12. Anders Nygren, *Agape and Eros* (New York: Harper and Row, 1969), 712-13, cited by Gudorf, "Parenting, Mutual Love, and Sacrifice," 182.

13. Horace Bushnell, *The Vicarious Sacrifice, Grounded in Principles of Universal Obligation* (New York, 1866), in Horace Bushnell, ed. H. Shelton Smith (New York: Oxford University Press, 1965), 282, cited by Ann Taves, "Mothers and Children and the legacy of Mid-19th Century American Christianity," *The Journal of Religion* 67, no. 2 (April 1987):206.

14. Henry Ward Beecher, *Royal Truth* (Boston, 1866), cited by Taves, "Mothers and Children," 207.

15. Rita Nakashima Brock, *Journeys by Heart: A Christology of Erotic Power* (New York: Crossroad, 1988), xii, 3, 50, 53, 56, 69, 70.

16. Joanne Carlson Brown and Rebecca Parker, "For God So Loved the World," *Violence against Women and Children: A Christian Theological Handbook*, ed. Carol J. Adams and Marie M. Fortune (New York: Continuum, 1995), 55, 56.

17. Brown and Parker, "For God So Loved the World," 56. See Carter Heyward, *The Redemption of God: A Theology of Mutual Relation* (Washington, D.C.: University Press of America, 1982) and Rosemary Radford Ruether, *Sexism and God-Talk: Toward a Feminist Theology* (Boston: Beacon, 1983).

18. See Bonnie J. Miller-McLemore, "Sloppy Mutuality: Love and Justice for Children and Adults," *Mutuality Matters: Faith, Family and Just Love*, ed. Edward Foley, et al. (Lanham: Sheed & Ward, 2004), 127-128, and Don S. Browning, et al., *From Culture Wars to Common Ground: Religion and the American Family Debate* (Louisville: Westminster John Knox, 1997), 273.

19. Brita L. Gill-Austern, "Love Understood as Self-Sacrifice and Self-Denial: What Does It Do to Women?" in *Through the Eyes of Women: Insights for Pastoral Care,* ed. Jeanne Stevenson Moessner (Minneapolis: Augsburg Fortress, 1996), 318.

20. Miller-McLemore, *Also a Mother*, 152-153 and Herbert Anderson and Susan B. W. Johnson, *Regarding Children: A New Respect for Childhood and Families* (Louisville: Westminster John Knox, 1994), 27. The phrase comes from Gen. 33:14.

21. Lisa Cahill, *Family: A Christian Social Perspective* (Minneapolis: Fortress Press, 2000), xii, 6, 134.

22. Bradley, *The Power of Sacrifice*, 4, cited by R. Kevin Seasoltz, "Another Look at Sacrifice," *Worship* 74, no. 5 (Spring 2000):388.

23. Herbert Anderson, "Sacrificing Love," Sermon, St. Mark's Church, Seattle, Washington, October 19, 2003.

24. Gill-Austern, "Love as Self-Sacrifice and Self-Denial," 315.

25. Barbara Hilkert Andolsen, "Agape in Feminist Ethics," *The Journal of Religious Ethics* 9, no. 1 (1981):80.

26. Browning, Miller-McLemore, Couture, Lyon, and Franklin, *From Culture Wars to Common Ground*, 271.

27. See Pamela Cooper-White, *The Cry of Tamar: Violence against Women and the Church's Response* (Minneapolis: Fortress Press, 1995), 93-95 for helpful consideration of these points.

28. Catherine Keller, "More on Feminism, Self-Sacrifice, and Time: or, Too Many Words for Emptiness," *Buddhist-Christian Studies* 13 (1993):212, 214.

29. Daniel M. Bell, Jr., "Sacrifice," *New and Enlarged Handbook of Christian Theology*, ed. Donald W. Musser and Joseph L. Price (Nashville: Abingdon, 2003), 448.

30. Sharon G. Thornton, *Broken yet Beloved: A Pastoral Theology of the Cross* (St. Louis: Chalice, 2002), 70, and William C. Placher, ed., *Essentials of Christian Theology* (Louisville: Westminster John Knox, 2003), 188.

31. Anderson, "Sacrificing Love."

32. John Calvin, *Commentary on the Epistle of Paul to the Galatians (2:21)*, trans. William Pringle, in *Calvin's Commentaries*, vol. 21 (Grand Rapids: Baker, 1989), 77, cited by William C. Placher, "The Cross of Jesus Chris as Solidarity, Reconciliation, and Redemption," *Many Voices, One God: Being Faithful in a Pluralistic World: in Honor of Shirley Guthrie*, ed. Walter Brueggemann and George W. Stroup (Louisville: Westminster John Knox, 1998), 156.

Chapter 5

1. Bonnie J. Miller-McLemore, "'Pondering all these things': Mary and Motherhood" in *Blessed One: Protestant Perspectives on Mary* ed. Beverly Roberts Gaventa and Cynthia L. Rigby (Louisville: Westminster John Knox, 2002), 110.

2. Richard A. Shweder, *Thinking through Cultures: Expeditions in Cultural Psychology* (Cambridge: Harvard University Press, 1991), 1.

3. Alfred Margulies, *Empathic Imagination* (New York: Norton, 1989), xii.

4. Sam Keen, *Apology for Wonder* (New York: Harper and Row, 1969), 28.

5. Keen, *Apology for Wonder*, 29.

6. Carmen Bernos de Gasztold, *Prayers from the Ark and the Creatures' Choir*, trans. Rumer Godden (New York: Penguin, 1976), 51.

7. David Miller, "Held in mercy's hands," *The Lutheran* (September 2004).

8. Roland H. Bainton, translated and arranged. *The Martin Luther Christmas Book* (Philadelphia: Fortress Press, 1948), 12.

9. Bainton, *The Martin Luther Christmas Book*, 47-48.

10. Bainton, *The Martin Luther Christmas Book*, 69-70.

11. Gordon W. Lathrop, *Holy Things: A Liturgical Theology* (Minneapolis: Fortress Press, 1993), 11.

12. David F. Ford, *The Shape of Living: Spiritual Directions for Everyday Life* (Grand Rapids: Baker, 1997), 14.

13. Nicholas Wolterstorff, *Lament for a Son* (Grand Rapids: Eerdmans, 1987), 63.

14. George Stroup, *Before God* (Grand Rapids: Eerdmans, 2004), 16.

15. Margaret O'Gara, *The Ecumenical Gift Exchange* (Collegeville: Liturgical, 1998), 35.

16. Frank J. Barrett and Ronald E. Fry, *Appreciative Inquiry: A Positive Approach to Building Cooperative Capacity* (Chagrin Falls: Taos Institute, 2005), 25.

17. Kosuke Koyama, "Extend Hospitality to Strangers" *Currents in Theology and Mission* 20, 3 (June 1993): 165-176.

18. Rosemary L. Haughton, "Hospitality: Home and the Integration of Privacy and Community," in *The Longing for Home* ed. Leroy S. Rouner (Notre Dame: University of Notre Dame Press, 1996), 208.